T5-CFU-482

SUSTAINING THE EARTH: ROLE OF MULTILATERAL DEVELOPMENT INSTITUTIONS

POLICY ESSAY NO.9

SUSTAINING THE EARTH:

ROLE OF MULTILATERAL DEVELOPMENT INSTITUTIONS

MAURICE J. WILLIAMS AND PATTI L. PETESCH

OVERSEAS DEVELOPMENT COUNCIL
WASHINGTON, DC

Library of Congress Cataloging-in-Publication Data

Williams, Maurice J.
  Sustaining the Earth: Role of Multilateral Development Institutions/Maurice J. Williams and Patti L. Petesch.

Policy Essay No. 9
Includes bibliographical references.
  1. Sustainable development. 2. Economic development—Environmental aspects. 3. Non-governmental organizations. I. Petesch, Patti L. II. Title III. Series

HD75.6.W55   1993   338.9—dc20   93-5875 CIP

ISBN: 1-56517-011-3

Printed in the United States of America.

Director of Publications: Christine E. Contee
Publications Editor: Jacqueline Edlund-Braun
Publications Assistant: Elizabeth Easley
Edited by Linda Starke
Cover and book design by Tim Kenney Design Partners, Inc.

Contents

Foreword

The June 1992 Earth Summit marks a watershed in world affairs. This largest gathering of nations in history elevated the long-term security of the global environment to a priority concern for the international community. More than 170 world leaders committed their countries to pursuing strategies of economic development that would be environmentally sustainable. As agreed to in the conference's Rio Declaration on Environment and Development, ". . . environmental protection shall constitute an integral part of the development process and cannot be considered in isolation from it."

But this and the other commitments of the summit will remain symbolic gestures—and human and environmental threats will continue to mount—unless they are translated into concrete national and international policies and programs. At the international level, action on implementing the summit agreements has been slow. The lack of progress greatly reflects the summit's legacy of unresolved conflicts between the world's rich and poor countries over development and environmental priorities, and especially over the extent to which poverty alleviation is an essential component of environmental protection. Thus, while few world leaders doubt the need for increased cooperation in the transition to sustainable development in poor countries, agreement on priorities and financing for new development assistance programs continues to be elusive.

In this policy paper, Maurice J. Williams and Patti L. Petesch begin with the Rio conference and the lingering North-South tensions and then focus on the implications of the Earth Summit agreements for multilateral development cooperation. The study offers both a practical roadmap of the key multilateral institutions charged with following-up on the summit and an in-depth analysis of reforms required of these new and established organizations if they are to be effective in supporting environmentally sustainable development.

This effort is part of a continuing body of work at ODC on the relationship between eliminating global poverty and sustaining the environment that was launched with H. Jeffrey Leonard's *Environment and the Poor: Development Strategies for a Common Agenda*. Other ODC studies in this area include *Poverty, Natural Resources, and Public Policy in Central America* by Sheldon Annis and contributors and *North-South Environmental Strategies, Costs, and Bargains* by Patti L. Petesch.

The Overseas Development Council gratefully acknowledges The Barbara Gauntlett Foundation for their support of this study and The Ford Foundation and The Rockefeller Foundation for their support of the Council's overall program.

John W. Sewell
President
September 1993

Acknowledgments

Given the broad scope of this study, the authors wish to express their sincere gratitude to the many individuals who provided guidance on and support for this study. From ODC, John Sewell, Catherine Gwin, and Christine Contee gave essential direction to the project. In addition, the authors particularly benefited from the input of Warren Baum, Richard Bissell, Lee Kimball, Stephanie Smith Kinney, James Gustave Speth, Andrew Steer, Mahbub ul Haq, Gregory Votaw, and Joseph Wheeler. Also very helpful to the study were Carter Brandon, Herschelle Challenor, Erskine Childers, Nitin Desai, Luis Gomez-Echeverri, Susan Fletcher, Robert Goodland, Margaret Goodman, Patricia Bliss Guest, Scott Hajost, Twig Johnson, Stephen Kline, Michael Philips, Jane Pratt, David Reed, Katherine Sessions, Alexander Shakow, Ernest Stern, Peter Thatcher, Nicholas van Praag, Hassan Virji, and Alexander Wood. Finally, we wish to express our appreciation to Laurie De Freese for research assistance.

Summary of
Recommendations

The 1992 Rio Earth Summit and the consensus reached on the importance of sustainable development have given direction to future economic and industrial policies in every country. The 178 participating governments recognized that the economic progress of the past half-century was accompanied by ever-widening environmental degradation and that the development process of all countries required significant change. Industrial countries have to make fundamental course adjustments, especially in energy policy and the less wasteful use of natural resources. Developing countries need to accelerate development while both making it environmentally sustainable and spreading its benefits to eradicate poverty and to slow population growth.

The Earth Summit provided a vision of an interrelated process of sustainable development where the concerns for people, their livelihood, and the preservation of ecological systems are integrated in a global agenda of principles and practices—most importantly in Agenda 21 and the conventions on climate change and biological diversity. Agenda 21 created the framework for a new global partnership—for strengthening national capacities to change development patterns and policies—that redirects, as well as increases, development assistance. It assigns an important role to the multilateral agencies in this transition.

In recent decades, donor countries, including the United States, have pushed the multilateral development agencies to assume much of the development assistance leadership formerly provided by the bilateral agencies. This *Policy Essay* assesses how well prepared key multilateral agencies are to take the lead in effecting the transition to sustainable development.

The comparative advantages of the lead agencies of the U.N. system casts them in the following roles:

- the new U.N. Commission on Sustainable Development (CSD) will provide strategic guidance to nations and the multilateral development agencies on effective implementation of Agenda 21;
- the United Nations Development Programme (UNDP) builds human and institutional capacity through technical cooperation;
- the United Nations Environment Programme (UNEP) monitors and assesses global and regional environmental problems;
- the World Bank provides policy advice and capital investment for socioeconomic development; and
- the Global Environmental Facility (GEF)—cooperatively managed by the World Bank, UNDP, and UNEP—helps developing countries meet the costs of addressing systemic global threats to climate, stratospheric ozone, biological diversity, and international waters.

With the creation of the CSD, the necessary multilateral framework is in place, yet this review finds that the tasks and functions of each international organization need to be clarified, strengthened, or even established.

At the international level, industrial countries give highest priority to global environmental problems (i.e., climate change, species loss, and deforestation) and the need for shared responsibility. Yet the wide scope of Agenda 21's 115 action programs underlines that the world's environmental system is not separable into local, national, and international problems. Root causes of degradation at all levels must be addressed. For the South, Agenda 21 is important in supporting development that reduces poverty through economic growth and preserves the natural resource base. Developing countries also are more concerned than industrial countries that international assistance programs address local environmental problems, especially their rapidly degrading farmlands and their polluted water and urban air.

Agenda 21 calls on all nations to adopt national sustainable development strategies and calls on donor agencies to help developing countries build their human and institutional capacities to effectively design and implement their strategies. National strategies should redirect policies and investment programs for more sustainable development and reallocate existing resources of developing countries and aid agencies.

The multilateral development agencies provide about one-fifth of total official development flows; more important, they set the standards for development performance and lend coherence to the overall global effort of development assistance. It is therefore imperative that Agenda 21 programs become fully integrated into their operations. Through the prism of the respective key institutions, the remainder of this summary contains recommendations for strengthening the capacity of the multilateral development system to advance sustainable development.

U.N. COMMISSION ON SUSTAINABLE DEVELOPMENT: SETTING THE AGENDA

The new U.N. Commission on Sustainable Development was created in Rio to build commitment to, monitor, and mobilize resources for translating Agenda 21 into effective domestic and intergovernmental policies and programs. Without financial or enforcement capacities, the Commission must "nudge" governments and international institutions toward priority actions and an integrated set of policies and programs in those areas. As the Commission gets under way, it needs to:

■ Serve as *the* policy arena for building agreement on priorities for implementation of Agenda 21. The Commission's efforts to forge consensus, monitor progress, and mobilize resources on Agenda 21 programs should be principally organized around and guided by consideration of the sectoral issues (e.g., land management, forests, and toxic wastes) on the evolving agenda at the Commission's annual meetings, including review of essential cross-cutting concerns.

■ Help coordinate and rationalize intergovernmental programs on advancing sustainable development, particularly by setting priorities for and providing strategic guidance to the multilateral development institutions.

■ Develop reporting guidelines for U.N. system agencies and national governments to strengthen the flow of data and integrated analysis on environmental and development conditions and trends and to contribute to the Commission's monitoring of Agenda 21's implementation. Over time, the Commission should also foster dialogue and build agreement on norms and standards for advancing environmentally sustainable development.

■ Promote the redirection and expansion of international financial resources for Agenda 21 programs from donors and the multilateral development system.

■ Set new standards for the intergovernmental system on meaningful consultative relations with nongovernmental organizations (NGOs) in all aspects of the Commission's work.

UNDP: TECHNICAL COOPERATION FOR CAPACITY BUILDING

The United Nations is the principal source of multilateral funding of technical cooperation, with resources divided about equally between UNDP and U.N. specialized agencies, such as the U.N. Food and Agriculture Organization, the U.N. World Health Organization, and others. UNDP is at the hub of the U.N. system for coordinating technical cooperation activities through its offices in 124 countries and its close relations with governments. However, technical cooperation activities generally, and those directed by the United Nations in particular, are often criticized as ineffective in building the skills and institutional capacities of developing countries.

UNDP was designated by Agenda 21 as the lead agency for capacity building. It has taken a number of initiatives to raise funds and to help developing countries build their capacity for managing sustainable development. But, UNDP is short of qualified staff and funds to redirect its own technical cooperation activities and to implement sustainable development objectives. UNDP needs to:

■ Strengthen the number and ability of its professional staff to design and review capacity-building projects.

■ Accord highest priority to providing UNDP-administered funds to support the completion of national sustainable development strategies by developing countries for review by regional peer groups and by donors.

■ Revise its five-year core program to ensure concentration on capacity building for sustainable development.

■ Develop a design and evaluation staff or center to set standards of excellence in technical cooperation and to service technical cooperation operational activities of the U.N. system in areas of its comparative advantage, including capacity building in social and environmental sectors.

- Assess UNDP experience with human and institutional capacity building and give guidance on best practices.

UNEP: ENVIRONMENTAL MONITORING AND ASSESSMENT

UNEP has led the world community in monitoring and assessment of environmental problems. Over the past two decades it has played a key role in extending international environmental law. The agency's work has been outstanding in promoting cooperation among scientific and other professional communities to foster consensus on programs to combat marine pollution, climate change, and desertification. It also was UNEP-sponsored monitoring and assessment efforts that led to the Montreal Protocol to protect the stratospheric ozone layer, as well as to negotiations of the convention on climate change and biological diversity.

However, UNEP's Earthwatch database is incomplete and of varying quality. Much needs to be done to expand information for monitoring and assessing critical environmental trends in developing regions. Nor has UNEP been effective in coordinating environmental activities within the U.N. system—a task now assigned by governments to the Commission on Sustainable Development. Governments in Agenda 21 generally endorsed and sought to strengthen UNEP's ongoing programs.

To enhance its support of Agenda 21, UNEP should:

- Strengthen its role as the U.N. center of expertise for monitoring and assessment and for environmental law and major environmental problems, particularly those dealing with regional action in such areas as water, forests, and air pollution.
- Extend advice for periodic global and regional reviews of sustainable development progress and needs in support of CSD and the U.N. regional commissions for economic and social development.

WORLD BANK: POLICY GUIDANCE AND CAPITAL INVESTMENTS

The World Bank only began systematically to incorporate environmental criteria in its lending in the mid-1980s. By the late 1980s the

World Bank had adopted exemplary environmental directives and elements of a new environmental strategy. The World Bank's conceptual conclusion was that in most cases environmental protection and economic growth are compatible, or can be reasonably adjusted, given an appropriate policy and institutional framework. Policies are the key—particularly market-oriented policies. The strategy also places as much importance on institutional capacity building as on the World Bank's investment lending.

Both to support policy reform and to help developing countries redirect their policies and programs for sustainable development, the World Bank has expanded the scope of its technical assistance activities well beyond those associated with capital projects. In part, the organization is driven by experience, which indicates that well-directed technical assistance provides more effective means of ensuring policy and other reforms than does stand-alone conditionality.

The World Bank now requires all borrowers to prepare Environment Action Plans, which normally begin with an environmental issues paper by World Bank staff and are transformed into national environment plans comparable to national sustainable development strategies initiated by UNDP. Preparation of such plans is a principal recommendation of Agenda 21.

Although it is still early to assess the effectiveness of the World Bank's new environmental strategy, there are several potential weaknesses. The approach is overly economic and advanced in its application of market-oriented policies for environmental management, which to date have had quite limited application even in advanced industrial countries. This places a heavy burden on technical assistance for capacity building, especially since compliance on financial covenants in loan agreements has only been met in 22 percent of the cases. And the Bank is under serious constraints in administering technical assistance—limited staff experience, generally low priority for technical cooperation operations, and the high cost to borrowers of loan-financed technical assistance.

To improve its performance, the World Bank should:

■ Adopt an internal appeal and review process that monitors adherence to World Bank policies and procedures in project appraisal and implementation and provides independent reports to the Board of

Governors. A "watchdog" within the World Bank would assist in the transition to effective application of its recent new policies for poverty eradication and sustainable development, recognizing that the extensive new directives are well ahead of current practices.

- Ensure that the Environmental Action Plans it sponsors are compatible with the national sustainable development strategies (funded by UNDP) and that it collaborates with UNDP in their timely preparation for review by donor consultative groups.

- Mesh the application of "green conditionality" in its financing of sustainable development projects in developing countries with well-formulated packages of related training and institutional strengthening to ensure that recipients have the capacity for compliance with the desirable performance standards.

- Join UNDP in the work of the technical cooperation design and evaluation center recommended above. Both UNDP and bilateral donors should provide grant-funded technical cooperation to developing countries in support of World Bank sustainable development projects.

- In terms of programs, the Bank should reorient its work on the energy sector and step up its efforts on broad-based sustainable food production and on restraining population growth. In all sectors, such programs should seek to facilitate community involvement in the process of development.

GLOBAL ENVIRONMENT FACILITY: TARGETING GLOBAL THREATS

The Global Environment Facility was launched in 1991 with a collaborative institutional structure—involving the World Bank, UNDP, and UNEP—and a new "incremental cost" approach to providing concessional financing for projects with global environmental benefits. (The incremental cost refers to a partial or whole investment in a project that will deliver global benefits but that a developing country would not undertake on its own, such as establishing a park or using cleaner but costlier industrial technologies.)

Although the incremental cost approach and the innovative tripartite institutional arrangement were useful in getting the pilot project off the ground quickly, both operational and institutional retooling will be needed for GEF to move beyond the pilot phase and allow it to serve as an effective financing mechanism for implementation of the climate and biodiversity conventions and for any other international environmental concerns deemed appropriate. GEF should:

■ Selectively and flexibly apply the incremental cost approach in recognition of the fact that resources needed to address global problems cannot be entirely divorced from the kinds of measures and investments required to improve management of national environmental problems. The large overlap between national and global environmental problem-solving is perhaps most evident in the essential areas of capacity building and policy reforms.

■ Emphasize strategic and innovative investment projects. In the area of climate protection, increased attention should be given to energy-efficiency programs. In the area of biodiversity, participatory community development programs must be fully integrated into conservation and related land management programs.

■ Commit to moving beyond project and technical cooperation investments into the area of macroeconomic and sectoral policy reforms that will be pivotal to effective responses to global threats. Within its thematic areas, GEF should explore research and demonstration projects on the relationship between policy reforms and sustainable resource management as well as provide support for the technical aspects of legal, regulatory, and administrative policy reforms.

■ Seek greater autonomy from the implementing agencies for its operational policies and governing procedures. This would enable the organization to improve project quality, streamline the project cycle, and respond more readily to the guidance provided by the conferences of the parties to the climate and biodiversity conventions. The secretariat staff should be expanded and provide support for enhanced involvement of the Scientific and Technical Advisory Panel to ensure that project development and monitoring of implementation meets the highest standards. Also, it should be the exception rather than the rule that GEF project financing is subsumed within much larger World Bank lending programs that do not have global environmental concerns as their main objective.

■ Continued strengthening of GEF relations with scientific, environmental, and operating NGOs, particularly in developing countries. The restructured GEF should also remain committed to an open information policy and should improve consultative arrangements with NGOs.

In the spirit of the Rio Earth Summit, each of these key institutions must complete the strengthening necessary to ensure their effectiveness. Together they constitute the essential multilateral means for nations to work in concert for coherent management of their respective economies toward environmentally prudent and equitable global development.

Part I
A New Partnership for Sustainable Development

■ THE 1992 EARTH SUMMIT (officially UNCED—the United Nations Conference on Environment and Development) in Rio de Janeiro provided a vision of the seriously threatening environmental problems the world would face if it continued on the path of conventional economic development. The world's forests are growing steadily smaller, its drylands are losing vegetation, its topsoil layer is thinning, its waters are often polluted, and its plant and animal species are diminishing in number rapidly. Also alarming is the chance that increasing emissions of carbon dioxide and other "greenhouse" gases could produce significant and possibly catastrophic changes in the global climate.

The 178 nations attending the Earth Summit concluded that a change in the nature and practice of economic growth and development is urgently needed to deal with the ever-widening scope of environmental degradation. Consumption patterns in rich countries and the pressures of poverty and increasing populations on natural resources in poor regions combine to create an ominous threat to world ecosystems. In an increasingly global economy, the goal of environmentally sustainable development has recast North-South relations in the context of environmental interdependence and mutual responsibilities.

At the Earth Summit, the world's nations agreed on a set of principles and on a far-reaching plan of action, Agenda 21, to provide comprehensive guidance for fully integrating the environmental dimensions into the economic policies and programs of governments and development agencies.

Agenda 21 is the conceptual and programmatic framework for a new global partnership to redirect development patterns and policies for sustainable development. It is a partnership based on all countries' need to reform policy at the national level and to strengthen capacities to improve environmental management. For developing regions, the complexity and magnitude of the task necessarily focused attention on the important role of development assistance, both in terms of its volume and its redirection toward sustainable development.

ASSISTANCE FOR SUSTAINABLE DEVELOPMENT

■ THE VOLUME OF AID and the institutional channels for providing it were major concerns at the Earth Summit. Preliminary UNCED estimates of the cost to developing countries of implementing Agenda 21's plan for accelerated economic growth on an environmentally sustainable basis indicated a requirement of $625 billion annually to the year 2000, of which $500 billion would be financed by developing countries' own resources. The remaining $125 billion a year, required from external sources, is well in excess of the $73 billion of development finance (of which $57 billion was concessional official development assistance, or ODA) provided to all developing countries in 1991.[1]

Clearly, a major mobilization of financial resources is needed to respond to developing-country priorities as they complete national sustainable development strategies and expand their capacities for effective implementation of Agenda 21. Unfortunately, efforts at the Earth Summit to obtain advance assurances of increased financial assistance yielded ambiguous results. Industrial countries have not been more forthcoming with additional funds because, in part, of recognition that developing countries cannot effectively expand sustainable development programs without first a good deal of retooling of existing policies and practices, reforms that Agenda 21 strongly emphasized.

It is also clear that under existing conditions of economic recession and budgetary stringency, a substantial portion of new funding must come from redeployment of existing resources, in both industrial and developing countries, as well as from a reshaping of current policies and fiscal practices so as to provide positive incentives for investment in sustainable development from private as well as public sources.

This *Policy Essay* concentrates on the role of official development assistance as directed by multilateral institutions to help developing countries implement Agenda 21. Past Cold War development assistance criteria are changing, and Agenda 21, in effect, calls for a departure from traditional notions of "foreign aid" in favor of a new global partnership for the transition to sustainable development. It also assigns the multilateral agencies a leading role in this transition.

. . . .
KEY MULTILATERAL AGENCIES

■ ALTHOUGH THE MULTILATERAL AGENCIES only provide about 20 percent of total official flows, they are looked to by the major bilateral donors to set standards for development performance and to lend coherence to the overall global effort of development assistance. As a consequence, the multilateral assistance institutions exert major influence on development policies and practices throughout the world.

The central question addressed in this *Policy Essay*, following a review of the agreements made in Rio, is whether U.N. agencies and the multilateral development institutions—collectively and individually—are up to the task of leading the transition to sustainable development.

With the establishment of the United Nations Commission on Sustainable Development (CSD), the requisite institutional structure of key multilateral agencies appears to be in place:

■ The U.N. Commission on Sustainable Development will provide strategic guidance to the world community on effective implementation of Agenda 21.

■ The United Nations Development Programme (UNDP) is the lead agency for technical assistance on building human and institutional capacities for sustainable development, drawing on the relevant specialized agencies and programs of the United Nations.

■ The United Nations Environment Programme (UNEP) is charged with monitoring and assessing the critical state of global and regional environment problems and the adequacy of instruments to deal with them.

■ The World Bank is the lead international institution for policy advice, for appraisal of national investment requirements for socioeconomic development, and for mobilization of the means for meeting these needs (with the regional development banks playing an important complementary role).

■ The Global Environment Facility (GEF) is the mechanism in the international development system for coordinated delivery of aid to reduce greenhouse gas emissions and ozone layer depletion and to protect biological diversity and international waters.

Although the institutional map appears adequate, there is a need to clarify roles, strengthen particular approaches and capacities, and ensure that the relationships among the major agencies are mutually reinforcing if the organizations are to help meet the objectives agreed to by the 178 governments at the Earth Summit.

Part II
Agreements Adopted at the Earth Summit

■ THE NEGOTIATED PRODUCTS OF THE SUMMIT were the Rio Declaration on Environment and Development and Agenda 21. Additionally, two separately negotiated and legally binding conventions, aimed at slowing global climate change and conserving biological diversity, were each signed by more than 150 governments at the Earth Summit. Governments also adopted a statement of principles on forests as the basis of a possible future convention.

. . . .

THE RIO DECLARATION

■ SUSTAINABLE DEVELOPMENT has been described as meeting the needs of the present generation without jeopardizing the ability of future generations to meet their own needs.[2] The Rio Declaration seeks to make that concept operable in a covenant of 27 carefully negotiated principles on the relationship of environment and development. Agreement on such norms and standards is important to facilitate a consensus on the nature of sustainable development problems and acceptable patterns of international conduct.

Among the important principles and norms agreed are[3]:

■ the sovereign right of states to exploit their own resources provided that activities within their own borders do not cause damage beyond,

■ the importance of precautionary actions to limit the risks of environmental damage before it occurs,

■ the need to codify in law the liability of polluters to compensate for environmental damage,

■ the principle of shared but differentiated responsibilities among rich and poor nations, and

■ an emphasis on the "eradication of poverty" and "decreasing disparities in standards of living."

....
THE CONVENTIONS

■ THE CONVENTIONS ON CLIMATE change and biological diversity focus on two urgent global problems that can only be effectively addressed by cooperation among a broad spectrum of countries. To help economically weak countries meet the obligations incurred, additional financial assistance is required.

The Framework Convention on Climate Change is important as the first international legal instrument to recognize global warming as a threat to the planet. Its parties are committed to the goal of stabilizing greenhouse gas concentrations in the atmosphere at a level that would prevent a dangerous change in the earth's climate, and to do so in a time frame that will permit ecosystems to adapt to any unavoidable change. The parties agreed to develop national mitigating programs addressing emissions of greenhouse gases.

Widely discussed, but not agreed during the negotiations, was a proposal to reduce carbon dioxide emissions to 1990 levels by the year 2000, a target opposed by the United States under the Bush administration. President Clinton has indicated that the United States will now sign the convention and will seek international agreement to such a target within that framework.

The Convention on Biological Diversity calls for national strategies for the conservation and sustainable use of plant and animal species and for inventories of species as a basis for consumption objectives and policies. Species diversity today is found largely in developing countries. Under the convention, access to genetic resources—formerly unrestricted—will be subject to the prior consent of the supplying country on "mutually agreed terms."

Most industrial-country governments joined with developing countries in signing the biological diversity convention, but they reserved their right to clarify provisions covering intellectual property rights and the mechanism for determining levels and priorities of aid to developing-country conservation efforts. Because of similar concerns, the United States did not sign the convention in Rio, but under the Clinton administration it did so in June 1993.

Both conventions address issues closely related to key elements of Agenda 21's comprehensive plan of action.

. . . .

AGENDA 21

■   AGENDA 21, THE MASTER PLAN FOR FOSTERING sustainable development in the transition to the twenty-first century, is a significant achievement. It is a pioneering effort to integrate environmental protection with economic development over a wide range of 115 action programs in 40 chapters. (See Annex.)

The advance in international environmental awareness demonstrated by Agenda 21 can best be understood by the fact that before 1990, most developing-country officials viewed with suspicion Northern concern about the environment. Some openly avowed that they welcomed the pollution of industrialization. Others saw concerns with conservation of wildlife as an unfortunate diversion from development efforts. "People before pandas" was a common slogan of Southern representatives.

Moreover, most industrial countries and development assistance agencies in the pre-UNCED period had done little to apply environmental criteria to development; and some of their actions were directly harmful. The 1990 report on development cooperation of the Organisation for Economic Co-operation and Development (OECD) states that most aid agencies "have gone much further in the articulation of environmental policy than they have in its implementation."[4]

Many aid projects billed as "environmental" mainly involved reclassification of projects in traditional areas such as water supply and sanitation, forestry, soil conservation, and rural development. Although this recognition of the natural-resource base of development may have been helpful, the environmental problem generally was seen more in terms of mitigating the adverse effects of resource degradation than in terms of dealing with root causes. Few aid projects addressed the environmental effects of urbanization and industrial development, and training of developing-country officials in environmental management was in its infancy.

Agenda 21 seeks to remedy this relative neglect of environmental considerations. It includes some of the best current thinking on sustainable development. A mix of general principles and proposed programs, Agenda 21 emphasizes, for example, the desirability of more participatory approaches to decisionmaking, the important role of women, the application of market incentives, avoidance of subsidies that encourage waste, and the necessity for environmental legislation and assessments.

Governments at the Earth Summit generally accepted that the damage that current development patterns inflict on the natural resource base requires adjustment of goals and methods. But they disagreed about possible "limits" in such areas as the use of energy in affluent societies, about population growth in developing regions, about rates of forestry depletion, and about the extent to which poverty eradication should be accorded priority as an environmental concern. These were difficult and contentious issues in the negotiations of Agenda 21—issues that were glossed over by consensus diplomacy and remain largely unresolved.

As the Agenda 21 negotiations proceeded, however, participants sought to push beyond traditional approaches in recognition that environmental sustainability required dealing not only with the symptoms but with deeper causes as well. Contributing to this understanding was the growing concern that environmental degradation was beginning to affect global systems that support life on earth.

SYSTEMIC GLOBAL AND NATIONAL ISSUES

In the 1970s it became clear that environmental problems extended beyond local communities, and that across borders nations shared such environmental problems as polluted rivers and water bodies, acid rain, and the need to protect migratory and endangered species. International meetings in these areas set the stage for the more comprehensive global environmental treaties, including the Montreal Protocol on Substances That Deplete the Ozone Layer and the Convention on Trade in Endangered Species.

The imperatives for transnational management of global environmental problems are changing the nature of international relations, since the North needs the cooperation of the South to deal effectively with such systemic global problems as climate change, transboundary pollution, and depletion of the ozone layer. Critical to better management is the new concept of "shared but differentiated responsibility," which recognizes important differences in the responsibilities of states for environmental problems and in their capacities to contribute to solutions. Implicitly recognized is that industrial countries have a major responsibility for both aspects.

These global environmental threats most concerned the industrial countries at the Earth Summit and received priority attention. The immediate environmental threats affecting the health and well-being of large populations in the developing regions, including poisoned water supplies, unsanitary health conditions, and rapidly degrading soils, received relatively less consideration.

Underlying Agenda 21 is the view that the world's environment is indivisible and that dealing effectively with global environmental problems will require dealing with the root causes of environmental degradation at the national and regional level. This is the basis of developing countries' claim that programs related to poverty alleviation, drought, desertification, and deforestation should be accorded priority attention as problems of global concern. Since the Earth Summit, the U.N. General Assembly has initiated a process that could lead to a negotiated convention to combat desertification.

U.N. Under Secretary-General for Policy Coordination and Sustainable Development Nitin Desai sees the conceptual core of the Agenda 21 as being the program areas dealing with consumption patterns, poverty, and demographic pressures. "The objectives included in these program areas represent the hard core of the transition to sustainability," Desai argues.[5]

Agenda 21 briefly deals with the concept of "sustainable consumption" and includes an agreement that consideration be given to the "need for new concepts of wealth and prosperity which allow higher standards of living through changed lifestyles and are less dependent on the Earth's finite resources, and more in harmony with the Earth's carrying capacity."[6]

What this envisions is incentives to modify economic growth with production and consumption patterns responding to technological adaption and innovation. Although governments accepted this general principle, neither industrial nor developing countries were willing to adopt goals for its realization. U.S. representatives flatly stated that American consumption standards were not for negotiation. Yet without specifically agreed programs and targets for industrial countries, it is unlikely that priority will be accorded to accelerated research on energy and transportation alternatives or to adopting incentives for required changes in industrial and individual behavior.

Some developing-country participants in Rio questioned Northern concerns with population growth in view of excessive consumerism in the North and its adverse effect on the environment. At their insistence, Principle 8 of the Rio Declaration connected "reduction of unsustainable patterns of production and consumption" with promotion of appropriate demographic policies needed to achieve sustainable development and a higher quality of life for all people.[7] Agenda 21 recognizes that sustainability is fundamentally affected by population variables and it included a chapter on demographic trends and the pressures they put on development and the environment.

A central theme of Agenda 21, however, is the strong relationship between poverty reduction and environmental stewardship. In this case, Agenda 21 essentially seeks to combine two strands of development action: improving the poor's access to resources they require for survival and development and improving management of natural resources. Emphasis is placed on broad participation at the local level to ensure program effectiveness.

Most of the sectoral programs in Agenda 21 are closely related to poverty alleviation, including those focused on rural development, human settlements, health, and education. Addressing the rapid urbanization of societies will require enormous investments in services and infrastructure. Also proposed are programs for universal education, especially for girls, and for adequate nutrition.

Among the most urgent systemic environmental problems are those that cause illness and death on a massive scale in the Third World—dirty water, inadequate sanitation, and air pollution. Tackling these will require higher investments and cooperation in provision of safe water, adequate sanitation, safe disposal of wastes, and protection of air quality, particularly for low-income groups.

It is at the national level that concrete actions must be taken for sustainable development. Agenda 21 provides a comprehensive range of important programs but makes no attempt to assess priorities. Clearly the programs are not all of equal importance, nor can they all be undertaken at the same time. Moreover, each individual developing country must determine its respective priorities in response to the call for national sustainable development strategies.

But countries face a plethora of immediate requirements. In the two conventions, they are called on to prepare national programs to mitigate climate change and strategies for conservation and sustainable use of biological diversity. Agenda 21 proposes national forestry action plans (Chapter 11), strategies for sustainable use of marine life resources (Chapter 17), plans for promoting education (Chapter 36), and national capacity building strategies (Chapter 37). To meet many other such demands, assistance is needed to build relevant capacities.

The United Nations has seldom been an effective adviser on development priorities. Each U.N. agency and a series of conferences—on food, population, rural development, women, and children—calls on developing countries to adopt new national programs for the sectors being addressed. While all U.N. programs are important, the sequence of priorities remains elusive.

How do developing countries define a sustainable development strategy? What are the features of sustainability that will gain the political support of national constituencies as well as the financial support of donor agencies? At the international level, the new U.N. Commission on Sustainable Development can play a critical bridge-building role by advancing dialogue and mutual understanding between developing countries and donors about initial priorities and can provide a solid basis for the new "partnership in sustainable development" envisioned by the Rio Summit. Box 1 sets out a framework for domestic assessment of sustainable development priorities by developing countries.

BOX 1. ELEMENTS OF A NATIONAL SUSTAINABLE DEVELOPMENT STRATEGY

A sustainable development strategy provides a basis for identifying key elements that would almost certainly gain the support of development assistance agencies. Particularly important is a concerted effort to strengthen the professional and institutional capacities of developing countries.

While each nation will have to work out its own priorities for sustainable development, common elements of effective strategies should include the following.

■ First, environmental sustainability should be a major, explicit development goal, comparable in importance to growth in per capita income and improved social equity. Sustainable development criteria should be built into policymaking and regularly considered when investment projects are first conceived: at the outset of every major feasibility study and regional and sector program, and before macroeconomic policies are adopted.

■ Second, major public-sector expenditures should be screened for environmental impact, with particular attention to the possibility of postponing environmentally unsustainable capital projects, reducing subsidies that deplete natural resources, and scaling back inefficient public-sector enterprises.

■ Third, financing for expanded public-sector expenditures to redress environmental pressures should come from reallocating funds from unsustainable or less urgent activities, either before or as part of seeking foreign assistance for larger projects.

■ Fourth, training needs and the means for meeting them should be identified, because the present scarcity of relevant professional and management skills are as much a constraint as budget limitations. In particular, emphasis should be placed initially on building institutions and staff qualified to gather data and monitor environmental trends, to prepare competent environmental impact assessments, and to set standards for sustainability performance.

■ Fifth, increased emphasis is needed on mobilizing resources for Agenda 21 programs addressing poverty, safe water and sanitation, family planning, reforestation, land conservation, more efficient use of energy, and education.

Source: The common elements of the national sustainable development strategies proposed here in summary were originally recommended in "Economic Policies for Sustainable Development: A Synthesis Report Based on Seven Country Studies" (Manila: Asian Development Bank, October 1990), pp. 82–83.

BUILDING CAPACITIES FOR SUSTAINABLE DEVELOPMENT

Agenda 21 put major emphasis on strengthening the policies and institutions of developing countries for better management of environmentally sustainable development. This was recognized as requiring intensified technical cooperation (TC) to assist in redirecting current development efforts and assessing new investment activity.

Chapter 37 of Agenda 21 calls for special review by all governments and development assistance agencies of capacity-building needs and how those needs can best be met, including related issues of aid policy and management. Governments are asked to undertake "evaluation of existing capacity and capability for integrated management of environment and development; including technical, technological and institutional capacities and facilities to assess the environmental impact of development projects."[8]

Each developing country is expected to build a national consensus on its needs and priorities through a participatory process and to review its capacity-building requirements as part of its national sustainable development strategy. This also means creating capacities for formulating and implementing environmental policies, for assimilating appropriate technologies, and for building community support for environmental opportunities. Such programs would identify the key places in government and the private sector where environment-related capabilities need to be strengthened.

Agenda 21 assigns a lead role to the multilateral agencies to facilitate capacity building at the country level, and specifically to the "United Nations Development Programme, the World Bank and regional multilateral development banks, drawing on the expertise of the United National Environment Programme (UNEP) as well as the specialized agencies and organizations of the United Nations in their respective areas of competence."[9]

Part III
The United Nations and Sustainable Development

■ U.N. AGENCIES ARE DIRECTLY ENGAGED in helping governments strengthen their human and institutional capacities. In pursuit of this goal, the United Nations has the following strengths: expertise in various sectors; a field organization that allows close working relations with governments in the developing world; and an estimated $2 billion a year in grant aid. These capacities give the U.N. the means to strengthen tools for environmental management and to stimulate awareness of the need to include environmental considerations in development decisions at all levels.

The United Nations is the largest multilateral source of technical assistance. In comparison, World Bank funding of technical assistance has averaged $1.2 billion annually, most of which is related to investment projects. However, the proportion of Bank technical assistance has shifted dramatically from engineering type-services to focus on institution and human resource development. In this latter area the Bank accounts for almost half of the total annual technical assistance provided for similar purposes by U.N. agencies.

Despite high levels of aid, most U.N. agencies have not provided effective assistance to developing countries. Programs have been plagued by seemingly intractable problems of mismanagement, duplication of effort, and lack of accountability. This is due to the dispersed structure, overlapping agendas, diffusion of responsibility, and problems of competition and poor coordination among the numerous U.N. agencies. The autonomy of U.N. agencies and programs, with their built-in sectoral constituencies and governing bodies, has defied past efforts of reform and more effective program coordination. The result has been a loss of confidence by many governments and an erosion of financial support for U.N. development operations. A renewed effort at reform of the U.N. system is currently under way.

This reform movement reflects the new determination of governments to provide more policy direction for U.N. operations. U.N. agencies can respond to common goals when the priority is clearly recognized and enforced by governments.

Given the imperative of international cooperation in relation to environmental risks and the differing perceptions and priorities of how to deal with them, the essential role of the United Nations is to help governments build the political consensus to achieve new patterns of sustainable development. It is the United Nations' universal membership and its mandated concern to mobilize the world community of states and peoples to solve urgent social, economic, and political problems that provide the authority for monitoring and follow-up of the Earth Summit agreements.

．．．．．．．．．．．．．．．．．．．．．．．．．．．．．

THE U.N. COMMISSION ON SUSTAINABLE DEVELOPMENT: TRANSLATING THEMES INTO ACTION

■ THE EARTH SUMMIT NEGOTIATORS CREATED a permanent oversight body at the United Nations that would be devoted to monitoring and fleshing out the Rio accords. This newcomer to the multilateral community is the U.N. Commission on Sustainable Development, and its success will be measured by whether it can provide strategic guidance and build muscle over time to prod nations and the multilateral system into assimilating the broad Rio agenda.

The Commission's three major functions include: 1) providing a forum for debate and consensus-building among senior government officials on Agenda 21's implementation; 2) monitoring progress by international institutions and nations toward sustainable development; and 3) mobilizing international resources in support of Agenda 21 programs.

The CSD is a commission of the Economic and Social Council (ECOSOC) and will report its findings and recommendations to the U.N. General Assembly through ECOSOC. In December 1992, the General Assembly decided that the new body would consist of representatives from 53 states (with three-year terms), would meet annually for two to three weeks, and would be served by a small secretariat within the new Department of Policy Coordination and Sustainable Development in New York headed by U.N. Under Secretary-General Nitin Desai.[10]

The negotiation of Agenda 21 heightened international concern about environmental threats and their direct links to development, but the much more difficult work of translating that concern into concrete domestic and intergovernmental policies and programs remains. To spur action at the national level, the Commission can contribute by catalyzing reform and conveying information on how other countries are addressing similar problems.

Internationally, the Commission must maintain the momentum of change started in Rio to ensure that sustainability issues are considered at the intergovernmental level. To be effective, the CSD must especially help the multilateral development system sort out its priorities for action and must build agreement on a strategic and consistent set of policies and programs.

At a February 1993 organizational session, Commission members reached broad agreement on a proposal by the Secretary-General for a multi-year thematic work program that is grouped into nine clusters of issues based on the 40 Agenda 21 Chapters. The program themes are:

1994–1996

- critical elements of sustainability (Agenda 21 Chapters 2–5);
- financial resources and mechanisms (Chapter 33);
- education, science, and technology (Chapters 16, 34–37);
- decisionmaking structures (Chapters 8, 38–40);
- roles of major groups in the quest for sustainable development, such as women, indigenous peoples, and industry (Chapters 23–32);

1994

- health, human settlements, and fresh water (Chapters 6, 7, 18, 21);
- toxic chemicals and hazardous wastes (Chapters 19, 20, 22);

1995

- land, desertification, forests, and biodiversity (Chapters 10–15); and

1996

- atmosphere, oceans, and all kinds of seas (Chapters 9, 17).

The first five clusters are cross-cutting and will be reviewed annually by the Commission. The four subsequent sectoral groupings would be reviewed by the Commission (one cluster per year over the next 3 years) prior to the proposed 1997 special session of the U.N. General Assembly on progress since UNCED. It is clear, however, that even the issues within individual clusters are too numerous for consideration at a single Commission meeting. It will therefore be critical in advance of the meetings to set priorities and clarify a few major questions within the clusters for Commission members to debate. Toward that end, two ad hoc intersessional working groups were created at the June CSD meeting to focus on financial resources and technology cooperation.

The CSD's so-called thematic approach is a pragmatic one, and ideally the sectoral clusters should guide much of the Commission's work. It correctly focuses international attention on the substantive problems and, one hopes, their causes. And the review of cross-cutting areas should become much more meaningful in the context of the specific sectoral problems and needs. The ensuing debate on solutions should then lead the Commission to examine the strengths and weaknesses of national and intergovernmental institutions.

With a clear focus on each year's sectoral agenda, the intersessional activities of the Commission could benefit most from looking at 1) progress, problems, and priorities for implementation at national and regional levels; and 2) performance and coordination issues related to the multilateral development institutions, including U.N. and Bretton Woods agencies. The working groups must be able to draw on the technical expertise in relevant national ministries and international institutions (e.g., the national agriculture, forestry, environmental ministries, and Food and Agriculture Organization, the International Fund for Agricultural Development, UNDP and UNEP in the case of land management issues) as well as delegates from the foreign affairs, financial, and aid ministries and nongovernmental experts. These working groups will have to build the cross-cutting issues into their crucial work of reaching consensus on priorities for action and giving policy guidance to the CSD's annual meeting.

Through such a process, the intersessional work would bring together the key technical, political, and financial actors to focus on concrete problems. By extension, this advance work can contribute to the Commission's role to help bring greater coherence to and coordination across the development system.

Both Agenda 21 and the U.N. resolution establishing the CSD call for ministerial-level representation at the Commission's annual meetings. An indication of the priority that governments are investing in the Commission and its evolving agenda will be evident in the seniority and expertise of the delegations they send to those meetings. With commitment to action on global environmental concerns squarely on the agenda of the new U.S. administration, it is hoped that the United States will use the CSD to resume its international leadership on these issues. Importantly, Vice President Al Gore delivered a keynote address at the CSD's opening meeting in June 1993.

MONITORING PROGRESS

The Commission has been charged with overseeing multilateral and bilateral progress on the 115 program areas covered in Agenda 21 as well as to consider, "where appropriate," information on progress in the implementation of environmental conventions. Before the Commission can meaningfully fulfill these monitoring responsibilities, however, two major political and substantive hurdles must be overcome: the availability and exchange of data and analysis on economic and environmental conditions and trends must be greatly expanded, and countries must reach agreement on exactly what the Commission should monitor and assess.

At the insistence of mainly Southern governments in Rio, countries need only report on Agenda 21's implementation to the Commission on a voluntary basis.[11] There is great resistance on the part of these countries to model the watchdog role of the new Commission in any way on that of the more established U.N. Commission on Human Rights—also a commission of ECOSOC. As opposed to supporting public criticism of environmental practices, developing countries are likely to try to keep the work of the CSD away from close scrutiny of national performance with respect to Agenda 21.

Although the Commission should not become a forum dedicated to criticizing environmental protection efforts, the body should move forcefully on the essential task of developing norms and standards for assessing progress on human development and safeguarding vital global resources if it is ever to become an effective watchdog over and advocate of Agenda 21. As with its U.N. counterpart in the human rights field, it will take time and hard work to build consensus on indicators of what is and is not "sustainable." Moreover, tensions should be reduced to the extent that developing countries fully participate in the Commission's process of crafting reporting guidelines, analyzing development and environmental conditions and trends, and reaching agreement, if possible, on performance indicators.

The issue of information exchange and reporting guidelines received special attention during the Commission's June 1993 meeting, but greater efforts are needed before a substantive reporting process will be in place. As shown in Box 2, Commission members reached consensus on only very general reporting guidelines that span a broad range of issues and concerns.

Further work is required to ensure that the information provided to the Commission from countries and international organizations is comparable and can be readily synthesized and evaluated. For instance, Commission members requested information on sustainable consumption patterns and lifestyles, but there is no language on how these are defined or might be measured (quite obviously because there is no international agreement in this highly contentious area). Although inserting these concerns into the reporting process may contribute to advancing the Commission's policy dialogue, it is doubtful that many countries will give them serious attention in their initial reports to the CSD.

Of particular concern, attention should be focused on reporting related to the Commission's thematic agenda; and reportedly the CSD secretariat will circulate a questionnaire to countries on the type of infor-

BOX 2. U.N. CONFERENCE ON SUSTAINABLE DEVELOPMENT REPORTING GUIDELINES FOR THE SECRETARIAT AND NATIONS

Governments are "encouraged" to report annually to the Commission on Sustainable Development on efforts to implement Agenda 21, and the CSD Secretariat is required to do so. Below is a selected list of the guidelines for reporting.

■ Policies and measures adopted at the national level to meet the objectives of Agenda 21, including information on national sustainable development strategies;

■ Institutional mechanisms to address sustainable development issues, including the participation of NGOs in those mechanisms;

■ Assessment of progress achieved to date. These could be, where appropriate, in the form of statistical sheets or tables;

■ Measures taken, including indicators, and progress achieved to reach sustainable production and consumption patterns and lifestyles, to combat poverty and to limit the demographic impact on the life-supporting capacity of the planet;

■ Experience gained—for example, description of successful policies/projects that serve as models; particularly progress on strategies that improve both social conditions and environmental sustainability;

■ Specific problems and constraints encountered, including those related to finance and technology, as well as to the adverse impact of economic and trade policies and measures, in particular on developing countries;

■ Assessment of capacity that is, the availability of domestic human, technological, and financial resources;

■ Assessment of needs and priorities for external assistance in terms of finance, technology transfer, cooperation, and capacity building and human resource development;

■ Assessment of the effectiveness of activities and projects of the international organizations, including those of international financial institutions and funding mechanisms.

Source: Commission on Sustainable Development, U.N. Economic and Social Council, "Exchange of Information Regarding the Implementation of Agenda 21 at the National Level. . . ," E/CN.17/1993/L.3/ Rev. 1, June 22, 1993 (revised draft decision).

mation and data they could provide related to the 1994 thematic agenda on health, human settlements, fresh water, and toxic chemicals and hazardous wastes. Such a process will focus high-level attention on conditions and trends in those sectors. It might also usefully highlight strengths and weaknesses in national and international data collection and dissemination systems. In the longer term, the data might provide the basis for the formulation of useful indicators of sustainability or benchmarks by which to assess progress on Agenda 21's implementation.

Despite weaknesses in the reporting process, the CSD can—and indeed should—showcase selected promising national and multilateral initiatives at its meetings. However, it will be impossible in a two- to three-week meeting to do a systematic country-by-country or agency-by-agency review. As recommended below, peer review of national sustainable development strategies could be effectively performed under the auspices of existing U.N. regional economic commissions.

Ideally, the CSD should be able to say whether action plans, macroeconomic and sectoral priorities, and specific policies in reports it receives actually integrate environmental concerns and will contribute to sustainable development. As U.N. Secretary-General Boutros Boutros-Ghali correctly recommends in his report on UNCED follow-up: "Since the sectoral programmmes in Agenda 21 will be under review in relevant sectoral forums, the primary task of the review by the Commission on Sustainable Development must be in-depth evaluation, focusing on the linkages with other sectoral and cross-sectoral issues."[12] In assessing multisectoral and cross-cutting linkages, however, the Commission will need to navigate through contentious issues that are the jurisdiction of several sometimes rival bureaucracies (and public constituencies) at the local, national, and international levels. Another serious obstacle is that the secretariat's staff and budget are likely to be very small, and many kinds of expertise will be required in this effort.

Fortunately, the Commission will be able to call on a remarkably broad range of public and private institutions and actors to help clarify and implement its monitoring mandate. U.N. agencies will be reporting regularly to the Commission on conditions and trends in their respective sectors as well as on their efforts to implement Agenda 21. It will be vital for the Commission to develop close working relations not only with UNDP and UNEP, but also with sources of data and analysis outside the U.N. system. The World Bank and the Global Environment Facility, because of their key investment and policy guidance roles, are invited to submit reports as well as to send nonvoting representatives to the annual meetings.

Nongovernmental organizations (NGOs) have a vital role in helping the Commission become an effective monitor. According to a major new study on the effectiveness of international environmental institutions: "If there is one key variable accounting for policy change, it is the degree of domestic environmentalist pressure in the major industrialized democracies."[13] Public pressure for a better environment is also greatly on the rise in the developing world at the same time that southern NGOs are becoming active in the international policy arena.

At the Earth Summit and its preparatory meetings, NGOs from around the world contributed substantively to the official agreements. These groups closely monitored and widely publicized the UNCED deliberations, lobbied home governments, prepared draft language for the agreements, provided technical expertise, and participated directly on official delegations. Thus it is fitting that Agenda 21 contains a lengthy section dedicated entirely to strengthening the role of major groups— women, youth, indigenous peoples, NGOs, local governments, labor, business, scientists, and farmers—in formulating, implementing, and evaluating national and international Agenda 21 programs.

It will be particularly important for the Commission to tap into these groups for their acknowledged data-gathering capabilities; operational, technical, and analytical expertise; and knowledge of local conditions. Encouragingly, CSD will begin operations adhering to the accreditation procedures for observer status that were in effect during UNCED and its preparatory meetings, which are more open than ECOSOC's. This allows for more numerous and diverse nongovernmental participation.

MOBILIZING RESOURCES

Another major responsibility for the Commission is monitoring donors' financial support for implementation of Agenda 21 action programs and the conventions. Given the makeup of the Commission (i.e., that it will not include all the donors and that they will be outnumbered), donors are unlikely to use it as a forum for negotiating their aid levels.

The failure of UNCED to marshal increased resources from donors means that its reform agenda can only succeed by co-opting existing agendas and working within existing channels. To the extent that sustainable development means bringing environmental and poverty concerns into the mainstream of economic decisionmaking, the absence of large new financial resources should not be an excuse for delaying action. Additional resources, however, will be essential both to meet important needs and to retool entrenched ideas, interests, and bureaucracies in the international development system.

If the Commission is able to focus on specific sectoral themes, identify shared priorities, and build agreement on strategic approaches for multilateral action, then donors should be prepared to invest in those areas. The Commission will need to establish close working relationships with the U.N. development agencies not only to be able to draw on their expertise but also to help in this process of mobilizing resources. Such linkages can be mutually reinforcing; they will be especially critical if developing countries are to be active in the Commission and benefit from it.

The CSD can review, with the help of the OECD Development Assistance Committee, donors' financial delivery on the specific issue areas under its consideration. It should also be possible to assess donors' response in their bilateral programs to the priorities and strategies identified in the work of the Commission. Finally, the Commission should explore with private voluntary organizations and international businesses mechanisms for leveraging private resources behind its thematic agendas.

The Commission has both great potential to leverage change and important limits to its powers. On the one hand, it will provide an arena for high-level dialogue, public pressure (i.e., by providing channels for NGO views), peer review, expert assessments, and consensus-building on common norms and standards for advancing sustainable development. On the other hand, the Commission has neither enforcement nor budgetary capabilities, and its role as monitor is still to be defined. These are substantial weaknesses, and they reflect in part the low level of consensus in the international community about the kinds of policies and investments required to promote environmentally sustainable development.

The Commission's effectiveness thus depends crucially on its ability to "nudge" governments and institutions, both to deepen commitment to and agreement on strategies that advance sustainable development and to narrow the gaps between industrial and developing countries over priorities for action. To that end, the Commission on Sustainable Development should:

■ Serve as *the* policy arena for building agreement on priorities for implementation of Agenda 21. The Commission's efforts to forge consensus, monitor progress, and mobilize resources should be principally organized around and guided by consideration of the annual sectoral agendas, including review of essential cross-cutting concerns.

■ Help coordinate and rationalize intergovernmental programs on advancing sustainable development, particularly by setting priorities for and providing strategic guidance to the multilateral development institutions.

■ Develop reporting guidelines for U.N. system agencies and national governments to strengthen the flow of data and integrated analysis on environmental and development conditions and trends and to contribute to the Commission's monitoring of Agenda 21's implementation. Over time, the Commission should also foster dialogue and build agreement on norms and standards for advancing environmentally sustainable development.

■ Promote the redirection and expansion of international financial resources for Agenda 21 programs from donors and the multilateral development system, focusing on the shared priorities and needs identified in the work of the Commission.

■ Set new standards for the intergovernmental system on meaningful consultative relations with nongovernmental organizations in all aspects of the Commission's work.

. . . .

UNDP AND THE TRANSITION TO SUSTAINABLE DEVELOPMENT

■ THE EARTH SUMMIT GAVE UNDP the leading role in technical assistance to help developing countries build their capacities in support of sustainable development through implementation of Agenda 21. It is also expected to provide significant help to the Commission on Sustainable Development. UNDP is well positioned for this role. It is at the center of the U.N. system for funding and facilitating technical cooperation. About half these activities within the U.N. system are funded by voluntary government contributions to UNDP, which generally has turned to U.N. specialized agencies to carry out the activities.[14] The other half is provided by donors directly to the budgets and trust funds of the specialized agencies for specific technical cooperation purposes. At the regional level, technical cooperation is provided by the U.N. Economic and Social Commissions for Africa, Asia and the Pacific Islands, West Asia, and Latin America and the Caribbean.

Although it was once envisioned that UNDP should be the main U.N. conduit for funds for technical cooperation, neither the other agencies nor the donors have been willing to accord UNDP this degree of influence over operations. UNDP is largely staffed by generalists experienced in the management of financing technical cooperation, mainly looking to other agencies and consultants for project design and execution.

UNDP, through its funding and its offices in 124 countries, exercises a pervasive influence on the system's relations with governments in the field. Working with each recipient-country government, UNDP operates a system of aid programming that assists in identifying aid requirements and tabulates and reports ongoing aid projects from all donors. UNDP's own fund allocations are committed over a five-year cycle to each recipient country by "indicative planning figures"—a feature of clear recipient ownership in priority determination.

In this coordination role, UNDP convenes aid donor groups, known as round tables, for some 25 of the poorest countries to assist them in the presentation of their aid requirements to the donor community and to help them mobilize assistance. (Similar activity is undertaken by the World Bank, which organizes and chairs Consultative Groups for another 30 developing countries—those with relatively large capital assistance programs. The Bank looks to UNDP to report on technical cooperation requirements and methods at Consultative Group meetings.)

UNDP's annual funding is relatively small—about $1 billion with an average of 1,300 new project starts in 150 countries. It has an ongoing portfolio of some 6,000 projects.   The effectiveness of UNDP in fulfilling the role of advisor and coordinator of technical cooperation activities depends heavily on the experience of its country Resident Representatives. The professional staff are generally well informed on developing-country conditions and technical cooperation operations, and they play an important role in advising both recipient and donor governments.

Despite these assets and experience, UNDP's role in technical cooperation and its coordination has not been entirely effective, because of the decrease in UNDP funding and the quality of its Resident Representatives is very uneven. They have a dual diplomatic and development role in representing the United Nations—and political criteria often yield poor appointments.

UNDP has reduced dramatically its use of U.N. agencies for project execution, which currently accounts for only 30 percent of UNDP's project funding, in part, due to UNDP efforts to seek a sharper program focus away from past set patterns of technical cooperation allocation by U.N. agencies, and, in part, due to the objective of encouraging recipient countries to manage their own technical cooperation implementation. It is also true that the technical expertise of U.N. specialized agencies in many areas has declined (because of an overemphasis on operational activity) relative to that of outside organizations.

The technical cooperation activities of the United Nations are often criticized for poor quality and inadequate funding of an overly diffuse number of small projects lacking central program focus on and adequate attention to building the skills and institutional capacities of recipient countries—a criticism that UNDP has actively sought to remedy. UNDP has led the development community in evaluating the weaknesses of TC and in emphasizing the need of building self-reliant capacity by developing countries.

UNDP has built its own capability for direct project execution on a selective basis and has sought to shift its role and program focus on the strengthening of developing-country capacities to manage all aspects of the development process. This concept imbues a wide range of UNDP-financed activities, including a Management Development Programme. As part of enhancing the capacity of developing countries, UNDP has been gradually expanding recipient execution of technical cooperation projects, in sharp contrast with its past practice of favoring external executing agents, which are now seen as weakening national capabilities and responsibility.

UNDP's annual *Human Development Report* has focused world-wide attention on human and institutional assistance and has strengthened support of UNDP as the lead agency for carrying out a principal objective of Agenda 21, namely the building of developing-country capacities for environmentally sustainable development.

UNDP'S RESPONSE TO THE EARTH SUMMIT

In 1988, UNDP established an Environment Action Team that launched several innovative initiatives in preparation for and follow-up of the Earth Summit, including:

■ a series of workshops and training seminars on environment and development, with an emphasis on field staff cooperation with NGOs;

■ formulation of Environment Management Guidelines to provide a systematic framework for integrating the environment dimension into programming and project design;

■ a pilot project of 35 national and regional centers within a Sustainable Development Network (SDN) to make relevant information available by electronic means to officials and groups directly concerned with the planning for the project done by personnel of official agencies, research institutes, and NGOs.

■ cooperation in the preparation of national environmental reports requested by the UNCED secretariat on specific problems and recommended policies and programs, with UNDP Resident Representatives charged to stimulate the process. Although the 160 national reports received were of varying quality, they provide a basis for further work on the national sustainable development strategies called for in Agenda 21.

Prior to UNCED, UNDP was also a participant in a number of related special initiatives and funds. It cooperates with three partner agencies (UNEP, U.N. Industrial Development Organization, World Bank) in program implementation of the Multilateral Fund of the Montreal Protocol on Substances That Deplete the Ozone Layer. And it is actively involved with the World Bank and UNEP in the management of the Global Environment Facility, as discussed later. In cooperation with Arab states and Europe, UNDP initiated the Centre for Environment and Development in the Middle East in 1990. It also took the initiative to establish a Consultative Group for the Tropical Forestry Action Plan with an independent secretariat.

At the Earth Summit, UNDP launched Capacity 21, a fund with a target of $100 million "to aid countries in the formulation of sustainable development strategies and of required national capacity building programs."[15] Some $6 million was pledged by donor governments in 1992, and indications are that a total of about $30 million may be made available.

Generally, UNDP sees Capacity 21 as complementing and facilitating the capacity-building initiatives of existing programs such as the GEF, Montreal Protocol, and all UNDP-administered program funds. The execution of Capacity 21 is projected to be flexible, with UNDP relying on the expertise of U.N. system agencies (including the World Bank), bilateral agencies, NGOs, and private-sector and academic institutions. In line with its overall policy, UNDP seeks to emphasize national execution by developing countries.

Despite these promising initiatives, UNDP has been slow in follow-up implementation. Almost a year after the Earth Summit in Rio, plans for Capacity 21 were still under review and donors initially withheld funding pending clarification of the precise nature of UNDP's proposed Capacity 21 projects and their relation to its on-going programs. UNDP faced the dual constraints of a serious budget crunch—due to decline in donor contributions and exchange rate fluctuations—and lack of staff with capacity for environmentally related project design. With 25 percent of already approved programs on hold, including the previously launched Sustainable Development Network, UNDP has been in a state of near crisis.

The funding problem is symptomatic of more serious underlying uncertainties about reform of the United Nations, the organization's role in development, and—within this framework—the future of UNDP. No longer the central funding mechanism for the U.N. system, UNDP also lacks the staff for project design and evaluation to provide content for Capacity 21. The specialized agencies are pressing their own capacity-building proposals for donor funding.

An independent assessment sponsored by the World Wildlife Fund questioned whether UNDP has the technical expertise to include environmental considerations in its development projects and to monitor and mitigate the environmental consequences of its current and future funding activities.[16] Recognizing that UNDP is an agency entirely dependent on voluntary funding, the assessment places the main responsibility for fixing this on governments.

UNDP has consulted with its Resident Representatives and with developing-country officials on the formulation of project requirements for Capacity 21. UNDP's FY1994 budget includes a request for 41 national officers "dedicated exclusively to environmental matters."[17] Field offices are being encouraged to use existing funds to obtain technical advice relevant to their country programs. And the Sustainable Development Network is expected to provide an important resource in the 12 countries with initial pilot programs. By mid-1993, UNDP patched together criteria for the use of Capacity 21 funds to boost the environmental sustainability of all its activities on a country-program basis and projects that Capacity 21 will be operational in ten countries in 1993 and 15–20 in 1994.

UNDP has taken a number of promising and innovative initiatives with minimum staff and with program adjustments reflecting the decentralized nature of the organization. The emphasis on Resident Representatives and recipient countries for program direction plays to the agency's comparative advantage and political support, but UNDP still has to face the more fundamental changes required if it is truly to become the lead U.N. agency for technical cooperation and capacity building in support of sustainable development.

RECOMMENDATIONS: PROGRAM ADJUSTMENTS REQUIRED BY UNDP

■ UNDP needs to strengthen further its professional staff capability, both in the field by more consistently appointing well-qualified country representatives with development experience and by building up its central staff for design and evaluation of institutional and human resource capacity building projects. This central UNDP staff or center for technical cooperation design and review should be based on the experience of best practices; it should be seen as servicing and setting standards of excellence for the operational activities of the U.N. system as a whole and accepted by other agencies as a common effort. This also means acceptance by the agencies that they would compete for execution of technical cooperation projects on the basis of competence for delivery rather than the fixed share approach with country allocations of the past.

Such a central staff need not be large and could include secondments from other agencies to strengthen and ensure a common effort. Most important is that it be of top professional quality and charged to set standards of excellence in technical cooperation project development, execution, and follow-up evaluation for sustainable development. An independent review board of expert consultants should be constituted to meet periodically and advise on the performance of the central review and design staff.

■ While donors of technical cooperation grants may choose to continue dividing their multilateral funding support between UNDP-administered programs and the special purpose funds of other U.N. system agencies, there should be agreement on measures to ensure that the technical cooperation activities of the system meet standards of excellence set by the proposed review and design central staff of UNDP. It is not common funding but assurance of common standards of excellence that is essential to improve the performance of U.N. agencies in building human and institutional capacities.

■ UNDP's budget allocations in the five-year indicative planning figures should be reviewed with country recipients to gain acceptance of an integrated focus on capacity building for sustainable development, and its five-year program reoriented accordingly.

■ UNDP Resident Representatives, in consultation with developing-country officials, should determine what needs to be done to assure initial completion of national sustainable development strategies, to be followed by review meetings of both regional peer groups and donors. Support for completion and successive updating of national sustainable development strategies should have first call on Capacity 21 administered funds. As sustainable development activities focused on capacity building are fully integrated in programs supported by UNDP, the need for a separate fund to jump-start post-Rio collaborative activities will diminish and the focus should be on more adequate funding of UNDP and related activities as a whole.

■ UNDP experience and best practices on human and institutional capacity building needs to be analyzed and made available to guide all concerned and help them avoid repeating the mistakes of the past.

Progress with these reforms would go far to revitalize support for UNDP specifically, and the development role of the United Nations generally. It will require strong support by governments. To date, diverse forces within the U.N. system and administration continue to jockey for short-term advantage, and a kind of ad hoc process of piecemeal institutional adjustment prevails without an apparent clear vision of a longer term U.N. role in development. Without such a vision, confidence in the development role of UNDP and its funding base both appear likely to erode further.

. . . .

UNEP AT THE CENTER OF ENVIRONMENTAL NETWORKS

■ AT THE 1972 UNITED NATIONS CONFERENCE on the Human Environment in Stockholm, governments concluded that a special entity was required to ensure follow-up of a program of environmental assessments and management of corrective actions, and to serve as a "central catalyzing, coordinating, and stimulating body on environment within the United Nations system." In response, the United Nations Environment Programme (UNEP) was established in 1973 and based in Nairobi.

UNEP's areas of program concentration coincide with the technical agenda of UNCED, namely protection of the atmosphere, management of fresh water and oceans, terrestrial ecosystems and their resources, biological diversity, toxic chemicals and waste management, and environmental law and policy.

With a relatively small secretariat and a limited budget, UNEP has made good progress in laying the foundation for a global monitoring network and development of environmental law and policy, but it has largely failed in its mandate of environmental coordination within the United Nations. Governments at the Earth Summit recognized the necessity for a stronger institutional approach to U.N. coordination by creating the Commission on Sustainable Development.

Although they reduced UNEP's coordinating function, governments otherwise endorsed UNEP's ongoing programs. The overall effect has been to reinforce UNEP's existing role with some changes in emphasis, rather than major changes in its program.

GLOBAL MONITORING AND EVALUATION NETWORKS

UNEP has stressed that a key to dealing with environmental problems is generating scientifically reliable information and well-founded assessments. Its annual reviews on key conditions and environmental trends are largely drawn from "Earthwatch," a loose affiliation of U.N. research and monitoring programs. Within UNEP, this encompasses the Global Environment Monitoring System (GEMS), the Global Resource Information Database (GRID), the International Registry of Potentially Toxic Chemicals (IRPTC), and the Global Atmosphere Watch. Earthwatch also includes World Health Organization (WHO) assessments on water and other factors affecting health and by Food and Agriculture Organization (FAO) and U.N. Educational, Scientific, and Cultural Organization (UNESCO) on natural resources. Its assessments are widely distributed through cooperative publication arrangements.

UNEP's Environment Fund encourages the strengthening of monitoring and assessment functions of the United Nations and of contributing agencies, as well as maintaining a worldwide referral system of more than 140 national focal points (INFOTERRA) as a clearing house for exchanges of information.

The Earthwatch data base is of varing quality, however, often fragmented and incomplete, and much needs to be done to strengthen the collaboration of the agencies and programs contributing to it and to ensure that countries have the technical capacity to use the information that is available. Moreover, there is a particular lack of information about the environment in developing regions. In most sectors, the data on regional and global trends also provide an insufficient basis for policy evaluation. This is the case, for example, concerning the oceans as sinks for wastes and for absorbing greenhouse gases, which is a major factor of uncertainty in determining the prospect of climate change. On land, there are conflicting data on the scale and rate of natural resource degradation.

CONTRIBUTIONS OF SCIENTIFIC AND OTHER PROFESSIONAL COMMUNITIES

To promote technical and programmatic contributions by scientific and other professional communities, UNEP—in collaboration with other U.N. agencies—commissioned independent experts to foster consensus on controversial policy matters such as marine pollution, desertification, and climate change. The programs received inputs from operating agencies of the United Nations and their counterparts in national governments in cooperation with the scientific community.

UNEP has maintained close relations with the major networks of scientific organizations and generally engaged their active support on key environmental problems. Of particular importance is the Global Change System for Analysis, Research, and Training (START), of the International Geosphere-Biosphere Program, the World Climate Research Program, and the Human Dimensions of Global Environmental Change Program in cooperation with associated scientific organizations. START seeks to address inadequacies in the current distribution of scientific and technological expertise through a global network of regional research centers doing fundamental research and training in the earth sciences.

START promotes interdisciplinary studies in all major regional ecosystems on land, coastal areas, and the open seas. It also helps strengthen research capabilities in global change science and encourages developing countries to use those resources. Priority has been given to building up regional research networks, centers, and institutes covering primarily developing regions. When completed, the system will enhance capacity and improve national and regional scientific infrastructure, in terms of both regional contributions to global change phenomena and regional impacts.

The promotion of scientific and professional knowledge about the environment and its contribution to the policy process has made considerable progress, and UNEP played an important role in helping to focus scientific attention and resources on critical regional and global environmental problems.

PROMOTING INTERNATIONAL ENVIRONMENTAL LAW AND POLICY

Early initiatives by UNEP and other international organizations led to the proposed "Action Plan to Protect Stratospheric Ozone." The resulting monitoring efforts and assessments laid the basis for the Vienna Convention in 1985, for the subsequent agreement for the total phaseout of chlorofluorocarbon production under the 1987 Montreal Protocol, and eventually for new institutional and funding arrangements.

UNEP, in collaboration with World Meteorological Organization, also led the intergovernmental negotiations on the greenhouse effect, which resulted in the Framework Convention on Climate Change. And UNEP provided the impetus for negotiation of the Convention on Biological Diversity.

Along with these international conventions, UNEP initiatives contributed to other important agreements on the transboundary movement of hazardous wastes and the protection of regional seas. UNEP also sponsored international meetings to develop guidelines and recommended practices on such topics as transboundary natural resources, land-based pollution of the marine environment, and the exchange of information on potentially harmful chemicals in international trade.

The monitoring and assessment efforts of UNEP, FAO, and UNESCO to deal with the problems of degraded natural resources, such as desertification and the loss of global forests, have been less successful in gaining donor support for significant international management programs—in part because of the cost of such programs and until recently its relative level of developed-country concern. Agenda 21 brought into sharp focus the importance of renewed efforts for improved management of ecosystems and their resources, including UNEP support of the preparation of the proposed convention on desertification and drought.

Overall, UNEP has been actively engaged in helping governments with the environmental policies, practices, conventions, and regulations that form a growing body of international environment law. Its environmental law program has made a major contribution through the legal instruments formulated on important problems and through a proven methodology and approach for extending international agreements. Agenda 21 has reiterated the major role of UNEP in further development of international environment law, and the importance of UNEP assistance in national efforts to establish and enhance legal and institutional frameworks.

UNEP AS A CENTRAL CATALYZING AND STIMULATING BODY

In its initial mandate, UNEP was charged with reviewing the impact of developing-country environmental policies and with assessing the costs of implementing national environmental programs. But UNEP lacks the staff capacity for work at the country level to assess such impacts or to come to grips with the economic and technology policies that affect them. Instead, UNEP has translated this responsibility into encouraging governments and agencies to incorporate environmental considerations in their development programs.

Before UNCED, development agencies paid little systematic attention to environmental impacts at the stages of project conception, design, and execution. Multilateral agencies agreed to a "Declaration of Environmental Policies and Procedures Related to Economic Development" in 1980, and a Committee of International Development Institutions on Environment (CIDIE) was initiated. The committee includes 16 multilateral development banks and the U.N. funding agencies UNDP, FAO, the International Fund for Agricultural Development, and the World Food Programme. UNEP was instrumental in launching CIDIE and setting up the secretariat, but follow-up was weak, and the committee never exercised much influence on its members' programs.

UNEP's efforts to introduce sound environmental management practices into the U.N. system were largely frustrated by a lack of systematic commitment within U.N. agencies. Indeed, that UNEP pressed the environmental cause led other agencies to excuse themselves on the ground that the responsibility for and costs of environmental programs belonged to UNEP. The organization, with its small staff, limited funds, and relative isolation in Nairobi, was largely marginalized by the major U.N. agencies.

The U.N. specialized agencies downgraded environmental coordination by discontinuing an Environment Coordination Board composed of the heads of agencies and in its place creating a middle-level committee of designated officials for environmental matters. While providing a focal point within their respective agencies for information, these officials had limited scope for program direction and coordination. All UNEP was able to accomplish was periodic discussions of specific issues and a report of current environmentally related activities throughout the U.N. system. This report, known as the Five-Year System-Wide Medium-Term Environment Program, purported to provide a framework for achieving environmentally sound development; in practice it was a paper exercise with little effect on the programs of agencies or governments.

UNEP has provided expert advice to governments in environmental monitoring, clean technology, education, and risk and environmental impact assessments, as well as helping to mobilize additional financial resources from donors. Although UNEP was not intended to be a financing or executing agency for technical cooperation operations—and does not qualify for UNDP funding—it has engaged in operational assistance and sought to enlarge its role as an operating agency. Almost half the UNEP-administered Environment Fund, averaging about $30 million annually, has been used for these purposes.

To summarize, during the past two decades UNEP has helped raise world awareness of the diversity and magnitude of environmental problems. It has led in development of important monitoring and evaluation networks, and it has played a key role in extending international environmental law as well as in promoting methodologies for management of global environment problems. UNEP has not been successful in its role to impel and coordinate environmental activities within the U.N. system. In large measure this has been due to the lack of cooperation from other agencies, but it is also true that UNEP has tended to diffuse its efforts and at times to exceed its capabilities.

RECOMMENDATIONS TO STRENGTHEN UNEP SUPPORT OF AGENDA 21

■ UNEP should concentrate its activities in areas of its established comparative advantage, as the center of expertise within the United Nations for monitoring and assessment of environmental trends and for expert advice to governments and agencies on major environmental problems.

■ UNEP should limit its engagement in operational assistance and drop activities that might best be carried out by others, including the study of potential political and military conflicts related to the environment and of an emergency response capability for environmental disasters. At the same time, UNEP's important role in identifying emerging environmental risks and impending natural disasters should be strengthened.

■ Governments should substantially increase assistance for the UNEP-administered Environment Fund in support of expanding the monitoring and assessment of critical environmental problems at regional and global level.

■ UNEP's work in environmental law and its expert advice to governments should be strengthened, particularly for regional environmental management activities, including those concerned with water, desertification, forests, and air pollution. It should also work closely with UNDP, which could develop regional action plans along the lines of the model provided by UNEP's Regional Seas Programme.

■ UNEP's regional offices should pursue transboundary environmental activities, such as those concerned with water, desertification, forests, soils, and air pollution. At the global level, UNEP's substantive assessments will be essential to the work of the Commission on Sustainable Development. Regionally, UNEP also should be appropriately staffed to help the U.N. regional social and economic commissions assess regional progress and programs, including peer reviews at the regional level of national strategies for sustainable development.

Part IV
The World Bank's Response
to the Environmental
Imperative

■   THE WORLD BANK and the regional development banks exert major influence on economic development throughout the world. The World Bank, in particular, has become the pacesetter for development policy, a role reinforced by its weight as the single largest source of official capital assistance. The World Bank was the first of the financing agencies to engage an environmental adviser in 1970 and to subject project appraisals to environmental criteria, although the practice has been quite uneven and a number of World Bank-financed projects have been criticized as environmentally harmful.

When in 1980 the development financing agencies adopted a Declaration on Environmental Policies, the World Bank held up its environmental procedures as a model. Yet neither the World Bank nor other development agencies effectively applied environmental assessments in their lending programs, and the Executive Director of UNEP was right to observe in 1985 that the "agencies have gone along with the Declaration in principle more than in action."[18]

In 1985 Congress passed into law recommendations calling on the U.S. Treasury Department "to monitor environmental aspects of Bank activities, to facilitate constructive U.S. involvement in assuring that sound environmental policies are implemented by multilateral agencies supported by the U.S."[19] Further legislation enjoined U.S. Executive Directors of the multilateral development banks (MDBs) to propose procedures "for systematic environmental assessment of development projects for which the respective Bank provides financial assistance, taking into consideration the guidelines and principles for Environment Impact Assessment promulgated by the United Nations Environment Programme" and to make environmental assessments, or comprehensive summaries of the assessments, available to "affected groups" and local NGOs.[20]

Only in 1986–87, during the presidency of Barber Conable, did the World Bank begin to take environment considerations seriously, and that was after a series of congressional hearings that illuminated the flawed environmental practices of the World Bank and other MDBs. U.S. NGOs were prime movers in mobilizing public and congressional attention to the failure of MBDs to pursue sound environmental practices, citing many examples of poorly conceived projects with adverse environmental effects, including projects in irrigation, hydroelectric power, forestry, and resettlement of frontier lands such as the Amazon Basin.

By the late 1980s the World Bank, along with the regional development banks, had adopted comprehensive procedures and methodologies for environmental assessments as well as augmented staffs and resources to implement them. However, incorporation of environmental concerns into their development programs is proving to be a slow and difficult process, because it requires a fundamental reorientation of the thinking and priorities not only of the MDBs but also of client governments dependent on development assistance. (See Box 3 for a brief description of the environmental policies of the regional development banks.)

· ·

REDIRECTION OF THE WORLD BANK ENVIRONMENT POLICY

■ DURING THE UNCED PREPARATIONS, the World Bank engaged in intensive efforts to strengthen its approach for dealing with the environmental aspects of its program. What emerged was a new and more effective strategy for integrating environmental protection into the Bank's decisionmaking processes—and those of developing countries— along the lines later agreed to by governments in Agenda 21. This section describes some of the limitations of the earlier World Bank treatment of the environment and the potential strengths and weaknesses of its new approach.

A particularly telling example of the weakness of the World Bank's earlier approach to the environment was provided by the Morse Commission's Independent Review for the Sardar Sarovar (Narmada) projects in India. A World Bank initiative for outside independent review of its projects is unprecedented; in this case, the review was commissioned by President Barber Conable in 1990. The independent assessment revealed "a history of omissions, unmet deadlines and ex post facto revisions" in the planning and implementation of the projects by both the World Bank and the Indian government, including absence of coordinated assessment and data for determining environmental impacts and a lack of resettlement planning for the people displaced by the project.[21]

The World Bank acknowledged that the independent review underscored the "importance of good baseline data and of effective consul-

BOX 3. REGIONAL DEVELOPMENT BANKS AND THE ENVIRONMENT

The regional development banks for Asia, Latin America, Africa, and Eastern Europe respond to the unique needs and culture of their clients and must be considered individually. By comparison with the World Bank, the regional development banks are smaller and, with the exception of the Inter-American Development Bank, lend significantly less money. Regional bank projects are often co-financed with the World Bank.

ASIAN DEVELOPMENT BANK (ADB). The ADB began environmental reviews of prospective projects in the early 1980s. Initially there was a team approach to identifying environmental problems at the project design stage. From this experience, ADB gradually evolved a set of environment guidelines and a sound process of impact assessment. Although its environmental staff has been small, and their role entirely advisory, the general effectiveness of the ongoing effort is credited with being reasonably effective.

In 1989, and again in 1990, the environmental unit was upgraded and its responsibilities increased. Currently the Office of Environment appraises the environmental aspects of projects and is responsible for environmental review during the implementation and post evaluation phases.

The ADB cooperated with the U.N. Economic and Social Commission for Asia and the Pacific in the preparation of a regional strategy for Environmentally Sound and Sustainable Development (ESSD), which was adopted by regional members in early 1991. Among the key elements of the strategy were: curtailing population growth, priority to meet the basic needs of the poor, changes in the life-styles of the well-to-do to promote sustainable development, and "measures pertaining to land tenure systems and land reform as a step towards achieving equitable access to natural resources and security of tenure ... and to tackle soil degradation, desertification and forest destruction." In these respects the ESSD strategy broke new political ground.

Most Asian countries prepared national reports for UNCED that have provided the basis for follow-up environmental action plans assisted by the World Bank and ADB.

INTER-AMERICAN DEVELOPMENT BANK (IDB). The IDB became aware of the environmental consequences of its program long after NGOs began calling attention to problems. As late as 1985 IDB lacked systematic procedures for environmental analysis, and it did not establish an Environmental Protection Division until 1989, as preparations began for the Earth Summit.

The procedures adopted by the IDB for classifying and evaluating environmental impacts of prospective projects are similar to those followed by the World Bank. An exception is the central role played by an IDB interdepartmental Environment Management Committee.

BOX 3. REGIONAL DEVELOPMENT BANKS AND THE
ENVIRONMENT (CONTINUED)

The IDB's *1991 Annual Report on the Environment and Natural Resources* notes that "the program so far has been very successful in assuring a high environmental quality of operations" and a new generation of projects. The report also mentions "the difficulty of preparing and implementing environmental operations in many countries in the region" and that "it is not enough for project documents to reflect the main environmental and social precautions now being adopted. These measures must also be properly applied in the field." Therein lies the major challenge for the regional development banks.

THE AFRICAN DEVELOPMENT BANK (AfDB). The AfDB has endorsed environmental policies similar to those of the World Bank but so far has not taken steps to incorporate them into its operations. AfDB does not require borrowers to prepare environment assessments for project proposals.

Nevertheless, the AfDB is closely associated with the World Bank's work on the environment. To aid countries in the preparation of environment action plans (EAPs), an environmental secretariat has been established in AfDB (in Abidjan) with support from the World Bank and other donors. The secretariat draws on the skills of Africans to provide training and technical assistance for preparation of EAPs. Most of the African countries are currently formulating EAPs and the experience so far indicates that their preparation can be slow and demanding.

EUROPEAN BANK FOR RECONSTRUCTION AND DEVELOPMENT (EBRD). The EBRD was established in May 1990; it is unique among the regional banks in that the bulk of its lending is targeted at the private sector. All EBRD members are in the process of adopting new environmental laws and programs. In comparison with the other regions, industrial pollution is the biggest environmental problem in Eastern Europe.

EBRD policies and structures reflect lessons learned from the World Bank, as do the environment assessment procedures. EBRD has a seven-person environmental unit concerned with screening all proposals for their environmental impacts, harmonizing East and West European environmental standards, and establishing remedial environmental programs that stress regional cooperation.

Sources: Asian Development Bank, Annual Report 1990 *(Manila: 1990); U.N. Economic and Social Commission for Asia and the Pacific,* Regional Strategy for Environmentally Sound and Sustainable Development *(Bangkok: 1991); Inter-American Development Bank,* 1991 Annual Report on the Environment and Natural Resources *(Washington, DC: 1992); World Bank,* The World Bank and the Environment: A Progress Report *(Washington, DC: 1992).*

tation of and participation by local people and the need for comprehensive environmental impact assessments and effective national and local institutions."[22] As the World Bank and the Government of India were unable to agree on the scale and timing for corrective action, the government canceled the loan, while indicating its intention to proceed with the Narmada dam on its own.

The remedy by the World Bank for this and other environmentally flawed projects has been to augment its environmental staff, expand its program of environmental research, and adopt more comprehensive environmental procedures.

The Environment Department advises on the World Bank's overall environmental policies and approaches; prepares working papers on natural resource management, environmental quality, and economics; and educates the country and regional staffs about applying sound environmental principles in their decisions on lending operations. The goal is to imbue the Bank staff with sensitivity for the environment. However, the Environment Department has no direct responsibility for decisions on the environmental components of projects nor for their independent review.

Responsibility for integrating environmental concerns into the operation of the World Bank rests entirely with the regional bureaus and country desks. Each of the six regional vice presidents has a regional environment division, and an increasing number of environmental staff can be found within country departments. The organization abandoned its earlier practice of having projects reviewed by the Environment Department at the end of the appraisal process, so that, instead, environmental concerns could be identified at an early stage of the project preparation process and integrated into project implementation.

An environmental impact assessment (EIA) of prospective projects is now central to the World Bank's approach for integrating environmental protection into its lending program. The scope and terms of reference of an EIA are jointly agreed between World Bank staff and the borrower, but formal responsibility for its preparation rests with the borrower, assisted by the World Bank. The regional environment division is responsible within the Bank for clearing the EIA. At that point the EIA's substantive recommendations, and the means to address them, are part of the overall appraisal of the project by the relevant country department.

The World Bank has identified a limited number of prospective projects to undergo environmental assessment on a selective basis. But in 1991, for the first time, *all* World Bank/International Development Association (IDA) loans were reviewed in relation to environmental criteria rating and almost half were subject to more detailed environment assessment. That same year the World Bank issued a new and enhanced Environmental Assessment Operational Directive and a three-volume Environmental Assessment Source Book to amplify the directive with "best practice" guidance and checklists for assessments in all sectors.[23] Thus, good environmental practices are becoming more routinely included in the Bank's operations.

A number of other directives deal with the environmental aspects of the design of specific projects concerning resettlement, protection of wildlife, and protection of indigenous peoples—areas of criticism of past World Bank performance. Also, a new forest policy was approved that shifts emphasis from supporting unfettered commercial logging ventures toward sustainable environment-enhancing practices. And the World Bank's program of environmental research has been substantially expanded. Thus, the World Bank has adopted exemplary environmental directives and procedures that should help to guard against the major environmental mistakes of the past. Still, the problem of environmental performance cannot entirely be met by directives, however well formulated. More fundamental are the operating assumptions of the World Bank's country departments when appraising projects and the attitudes of developing-country officials.

THE WORLD BANK ENVIRONMENTAL STRATEGY, THEN AND NOW

In the past, the World Bank has operated on the assumption that there is a direct trade-off between economic growth and environmental protection and that it is best to seek means to mitigate the effects of environmental degradation rather than deal with its initial causes. However, in the absence of an objective standard for determining an acceptable level of environmental damage, World Bank officials have usually compromised by seeking assurances from developing-country recipients that they will undertake mitigating measures—assurances that often proved false. The process facilitated approval of projects but the environmental costs have sometimes been high, as in the case of earlier Bank-financed forestry and land resettlement projects.

This approach by the World Bank has been severely criticized by some environmentalists who would have the organization apply absolute environmental standards in the first place and be much stricter with developing countries in enforcement of environmental conditions. Distrustful that the World Bank's new directives are mostly cosmetic, environmental NGOs continue to seek a more transparent information policy by the World Bank and an independent review process with mandatory power to block environmental abuses in projects. Some also advocate that the World Bank support environmental policy-based lending and conditionality to speed the transition of developing countries to environmentally sensitive development policies and programs.[24]

The elements of a new environmental strategy were outlined in the World Bank's *World Development Report 1992*, issued just before the Rio conference.[25] The report, drawing on the research work of the World Bank rather than its operational experience, comes to the important conceptual conclusion that in most cases environmental protection and economic growth are compatible, given an appropriate policy and institutional framework.

Policies that are good for both environment and development, according to *World Development Report 1992*, include removal of subsidies on natural resources, clarification of property rights, and investments in education and family planning programs, agricultural research and extension, and water and sanitation infrastructure. The appropriate policy involves correcting past market failures and distortions by price adjustments. These are the so-called win-win policies of the report. Different policies are required when there are negative links between growth and environment, based on assessing the relative costs and benefits of intervention and some means to reduce environmental excess—such as pollution and deforestation. Policies are the key in either case.

The new environmental strategy proposes reformed policies and more purposeful institutional reforms—together with the World Bank's investment project lending for the transfer of finance and technology. The emphasis on market-oriented policies for environmental protection is an adaption of the World Bank's established approach regarding macroeconomic reforms, and the emphasis on institutional strengthening furthers the institution's involvement in this area. The Bank has been moving in this direction because policies are only as effective as the capacity of institutions to execute them. Consequently, the new environmental strategy considers the World Bank's role in both policy reform and institutional strengthening to be as important as is its lending program.

The Vice President for Environmentally Sustainable Development with responsibility for the departments of environment, agriculture, and urban and water supply—a position created in October 1992—will guide the work of the World Bank in application of the new environmental strategy. As part of the overall policy for sustainable development, a new master directive on sustainable development is likely to be issued, one that will bring together the current thinking of the World Bank, not only for the lending program but also for research, country and economic sector work, and international cooperation.

THE WORLD BANK AND AGENDA 21

There are broad similarities between the World Bank's environmental strategy and Agenda 21. Both emphasize the importance for sustainable development of improved technologies and technology transfer, availability of additional financing, institutional and human capacity building, and policy reforms. Although the World Bank relies more on prescriptive, market-oriented policy reforms—and is inclined toward directive conditionality—Agenda 21 also emphasizes the importance of making major changes in private and public behavior and policies. Agenda 21 details sectoral programs and methodology for integrating environmental and economic considerations; the World Bank tries to achieve the integration by updating its operational directives.

Given the scale and range of World Bank commitments—$21.7 billion for 222 Bank and IDA projects and programs in FY1992—the institution can demonstrate activity in most of the 40 chapters of Agenda 21. Specifically directed to the environment are GEF-funded projects and an ambitious World Bank program of environment-related research. By the World Bank's own accounting, 19 loans, which totaled $1.9 billion, were primarily for environmental purposes (defined as projects with at least 50-percent financing or estimated benefits for the environment). An additional 43 projects had a 10-percent environmental component, similarly defined, and are classified as environmentally significant. The criteria for such classification are highly judgmental in nature.

In line with Agenda 21, the Bank's overall program emphasizes the complementarity between poverty and environmental degradation and includes commitments to expand poverty reduction programs; enhance the status of women through education, access to health care, and family planning; provide sanitation facilities and clean water; take account of population pressures on natural resources; and pursue broadly based economic growth that generates income opportunities for the poor. About 14 percent of overall World Bank lending falls into a new category of projects with specific interventions for reaching the poor or involving a measure of their participation. For IDA lending, the proportion is about 20 percent.

THE WORLD BANK AND INSTITUTIONAL CAPACITY BUILDING

The World Bank has fully accepted the UNCED conclusion that developing countries should undertake changes in their development strategies along the lines of Agenda 21, and that it and other assistance agencies should back up the transition by strengthening their own and developing countries' capacities for sustainable development.

The World Bank has expanded the scope of its technical cooperation activities well beyond those associated with capital project preparation and execution. For example, it has assumed an increasing role in the preparation of national studies and environment action plans (EAPs), the establishment of appropriate regulatory frameworks, and the strengthening of environmental institutions, technical training, and monitoring regimes. In part, the World Bank is driven to expand its institution-building technical cooperation activities by growing experience showing that well-directed technical cooperation is a better way to ensure policy reform than relying solely on the conditionality of policy-based structural adjustment lending.

The World Bank is forging ahead with its own approach to helping developing countries with building capacity to deal with environmental problems, somewhat in competition with similar activities of UNDP. Under the terms of agreement of the IDA-9 replenishment in 1989, low-income countries eligible for and requesting IDA lending must prepare EAPs that examine the causes of a country's environmental problems and identify the actions required to deal with them, including proposed policy, legislative, and other changes; investment requirements; institutional development; and education and training. An EAP process generally begins with the preparation of country environment issues papers by the World Bank's country department with support of its environment staff. They set the stage for and assist in the analysis for the EAP. While responsibility for preparing an EAP rests with the country concerned, the process was set up essentially to identify future economic and sector work and lending activities of the World Bank.

Indeed, the World Bank now seeks all borrowers to prepare EAPs and has expanded the scope of the reports in line with the broader national sustainable development strategies initiated by UNDP. As noted earlier, preparation of such plans is a principal recommendation of Agenda 21. In each case, the country planning approach—both the World Bank's and UNDP's—seeks to engage the participation of concerned local people, including business and industrial groups, NGOs, the scientific and technical community, and other interested parties. The plans also seek to include the donor community, both for their aid to country human and institutional capacity building and as a form of donor coordination. During 1992, World Bank-sponsored EAPs were completed by six countries, and some 50 others are now reported to be preparing EAPs or their equivalent.[26]

Many EAPs contain institution-building components, and World Bank lending supports a number of environment and technical assistance projects that are specifically designed to reform policy and institutional frameworks for environmental decisionmaking. In FY1992, six of the 19 primarily environmental projects approved by the World Bank were mainly concerned with building institutional capacity to plan and implement environmental strategies and action plans. The World Bank has also taken measures to strengthen its institutional development expertise, and research on technical assistance is being directed to focus on issues of capacity building. Additionally, a new Institutional Development Fund, initially for $25 million, has been set up on a pilot basis to provide grants to supplement Bank loans.

In summary, the World Bank now sees institutional strengthening or capacity building as an integral and highly cost-effective component of its new environmental strategy. Only by strengthening the institutional capacity of developing countries will it be possible for them to achieve a balanced and effective mix of policy reforms and industrial and other investments. It is clear that the early rationale for a separation of technical assistance and capital investment projects in separate institutions has broken down—particularly in areas of social sector and institutional development. World Bank and UNDP relations have been progressively closer in the last decade; these working arrangements need to be further solidified in partnership agreements, while recognizing the complementarities of the two institutions for selected operations.

. . . .

CRITIQUE OF THE WORLD BANK

■ ALTHOUGH THE WORLD BANK clearly has made great strides in its effort to integrate the goals of environmental protection and development, there remain several questions about the efficacy of its approach. First, does the Bank's project appraisal and review process adequately screen out environmentally flawed projects? Second, is the new environment strategy overly economic in its approach and too difficult for most developing countries to apply at current skill levels? And third, is the Bank appropriately equipped to carry out the institutional capacity building required by its new strategic approach? We consider each of these questions in turn.

As noted earlier, despite new directives for incorporating environmental considerations into project design and preparation, responsibility for deciding on the adequacy of appraisal rests solely with the World Bank's country departments. Effective changeover to the new strategy will take time, both in terms of rolling over the World Bank's portfolio to the new style projects and in retraining operating officials. It is important to remember that for more than 10 years the World Bank held up as exemplary in its earlier appraisal techniques and taught them to others when, in fact, they did not assure proper concern for the environment and the costs of flawed projects proved to be substantial.

The World Bank is now committed to providing prior information to the people directly affected by projects with large and diverse environmental impacts that it anticipates financing, which means encouraging full disclosure by the government that has applied for funds. This is an important step, but it begs the further question of why local consultations would not help the design and sustainability of all projects that affect local communities. The World Bank has admitted the need to do further work with borrowers in this critical area.

THE ECONOMICS OF THE NEW ENVIRONMENTAL STRATEGY

The economic policies proposed by the *World Development Report 1992* may prove to be operationally important, but to date their application has been fairly limited. In fact, they are well in advance of current practice in most advanced industrial economies, which have for the most part relied on command-driven regulatory policies in their environmental programs. Experienced environmental administrators believe that U.S. environmental policies should be recast to provide increased market incentives but recognize that this will require building political consensus and adaption to U.S. circumstances.

Similarly, the application of the World Bank's new environmental strategy will require adaption to developing-country experience. Institutional strengthening is the principal means envisioned by the World Bank for adaption to the new policies, combined with linking traditional investment lending with conditionality on environmental targets.

Growing demands on the World Bank to assure environmental performance come at a time when it is already heavily committed to a multiplicity of development tasks and is increasingly criticized for dictating developing-country policies and projects and for seeking to impose its views by multiple conditionalities on its lending. The result is that developing-country recipients tend to accept conditioned lending more from necessity than conviction, and they increasingly ignore World Bank-imposed conditions.

This situation explains, in part, the deterioration in the quality of the World Bank's loan portfolio as reported by former World Bank Vice President Willi Wapenhans in a special 1991 Report on Portfolio Management. Measured by such key indicators as economic rates of return and compliance with loan conditions, the report indicates that project performance by the World Bank was satisfactory up to 1973, somewhat irregular up to 1982, and declined sharply thereafter. Borrower compliance was "only 22 percent of the financial covenants in loan/credits agreements."[27] Market incentives pricing that the new environmental strategy of the Bank would seek to enforce would appear to be similarly difficult given the "conditionality fatigue" of many of the World Bank's clients.

A group of developing-country officials, selected for their experience and relations with the Bank, were consulted as part of the preparation of the Wapenhans report. They concluded that more World Bank-financed projects would prove satisfactory if borrowing countries felt they "owned" them. The group valued the rigorous analysis of the technical viability of proposed projects but felt that project selection and related policy options should be determined by them as borrowers rather than being dictated by World Bank staff on a "take it or leave it" basis.[28]

Given this experience, the Bank will need to link appropriate institutional capacity-building measures in most developing countries with environmentally sustainable projects. Although the Bank in its annual environment report points to a number of innovative approaches in select sectors and countries, with few exceptions, the scale of these efforts is as yet small. A notable exception is the European division's participation in regional watershed development programs. The Bank has administered the pre-investment or feasibility study stages of a succession of these programs that focus on environmental remediation and pollution control. Starting with the Mediterranean, the Bank has worked in the Baltic Sea, the Danube Basin, and now the Black Sea regions, identifying sources of pollution—factories, agro-industries, municipal sewerage—and recommending prioritized investments in new equipment, retrofitting, worker training, etc. In this case, the Bank's explicit operational strategy is based on a plan of integrated regional sustainable development, including step-by-step industrial reform and human resource training. In the case of the Danube Basin, the Bank has consulted closely with the 12 participating countries in formulating and running the Danube program, which is moving the former communist countries' industries toward compliance with the European Community's higher environmental standards and regulations.

STRENGTHENING INSTITUTIONAL CAPACITY BUILDING

Institutional building to support effective sustainable development programs must be tailored to the specific circumstances of individual developing countries, and since it requires a close follow-up in the field, the World Bank is not currently well equipped for the task.

The development experience of the last three decades indicates that effective technical assistance for capacity building requires sustained, "hands on" assistance in close proximity with client institutions. Particularly important is delegation of authority to the field for flexible adjustment of ongoing technical assistance, as well as for experienced inputs in the design of technical cooperation projects.

Moreover, the World Bank places generally low priority on technical assistance relative to capital lending. And its loan-financed technical assessments are much more expensive to its borrowers than the grant aid of the United Nations. In sum, the World Bank labors under serious built-in constraints in using technical assessments for institutional capacity building.

The World Bank is a highly centralized organization with 6,000 employees concentrated in the headquarters and only 100 posted in the field. The field representatives are primarily engaged as the liaison "eyes and ears" of the Bank in client countries and have no authority for on the spot operational decisions. World Bank staff are also more oriented to preparation than supervision of projects. As the Wapenhans report observes, the institution's inbred organizational culture focuses on and rewards effectiveness in the headquarters process of loan project design oriented mainly toward gaining approval by the Governors. There is little incentive for staff to focus on the problems or successes of implementation, although this may now be changing.

Although the World Bank is well equipped to handle traditional infrastructure and policy-based lending with its central staff—assisted by some 7,000 consultants at any one time—it is not set up for effective technical assistance in areas related to environmental and social sector institutional development.

RECOMMENDATIONS FOR THE WORLD BANK

■ The World Bank should adopt an appeal and review process within the organization as a second-line review of the judgment of country operating departments on project appraisals that are believed to be incomplete or faulty by senior officials of the Environment or other staff departments. Such a review by any one of its senior vice presidents prior to submission of the project to the Board would provide an element of safety for the World Bank against faulty projects during the period of changeover to the new strategy for sustainable development.

On a longer-term basis, the World Bank should consider appointment of a senior official, on a full-time basis, as an independent reviewer responsible to the Board of Governors for ongoing surveillance and review of staff adherence to policies and procedures in project preparation, appraisal, and follow-up execution. Such a "watchdog" function within the World Bank would assist in the transition to effective application of recent policies for poverty eradication and sustainable development, recognizing that the extensive new directives in these areas are well ahead of current practices within the organization in many cases.

■ The World Bank generally should pursue a policy of transparency on the availability of public information concerning the environmental effects of the projects it finances. As noted, it is already moving to implement a policy of giving prior information to those people directly affected by projects. Independent outside mandatory review of projects prior to Bank financing is not recommended, however, since such dual responsibility would not be viable.

- The Environmental Action Plans should be comparable in scope with UNDP-sponsored National Sustainable Development Strategies, covering the overall needs of developing countries for training and institutional capacity building as a basis for support by all donor assistance agencies. The World Bank and UNDP should cooperate closely in assuring the timely preparation of these country sustainable development plans and strategies for regional reviews by developing-country peer groups and for funding reviews by donor assistance consultative groups—while recognizing that the best coordination of all aid activities is by the developing country itself in the context of its own well-considered policies and programs.

- The World Bank should limit its application of "green conditionality" in its financing of sustainable development projects, stressing instead well-formulated technical cooperation packages of related training and institutional strengthening to ensure that recipients can comply with performance standards.

- The World Bank should work with UNDP on the proposed technical cooperation project design and review center, recommended above, and should help apply best experience in the formulation of technical cooperation capacity-building packages for sustainable development for both project and freestanding sector development. Grant funding of essential technical cooperation packages for World Bank-financed sustainable development projects should be available from UNDP-sponsored Capacity 21 as well as from bilateral grant assistance.

- In terms of program emphasis, the Bank should substantially reorient its energy and agricultural sector investment strategies. In its energy projects, it should move away from the emphasis on construction of large hydroelectric, fossil fuel, and nuclear plants and move toward investment in energy-efficiency programs and technologies, demand-side management policies, production of cleaner fuels, and use of alternative power sources. In agriculture, the Bank should step up its efforts to promote broad-based, sustainable food production at the local level.

■ Bank programs should facilitate community involvement, whether at the village or urban level, in the planning and implementation of its industrial and occupational projects. This process should be as participatory as possible, featuring "stakeholder" partnerships between federal and local government agencies, interest groups, and political factions. To achieve sustainable development, the highest premium must be placed on restraining population growth, and, as a corollary, investing in the empowerment of women in the development process, bringing them access to education, healthcare, and other social services, and ensuring their equitable participation in resource use.

Part V
The Global Environment
Facility

■ THE GLOBAL ENVIRONMENT FACILITY, launched in 1991, is a $1.3-billion three-year pilot project jointly run by the World Bank, UNDP, and UNEP. The facility makes grants to both low- and middle-income developing countries for projects that address four major threats to the global environment: global warming, pollution of international waters, destruction of biological diversity, and depletion of the stratospheric ozone layer. In searching for solutions, the pilot phase of the GEF was mandated to be "innovative and demonstrate the effectiveness of a particular technology or approach."[29]

Donors mobilized around the need for a special fund for the global environment with surprising speed, but the pilot program has been controversial since its inception. Some of the difficulties—notably the incremental cost approach (described below) and the collaborative institutional arrangement—are quite new and important issues on the international development agenda. In addition, GEF is struggling with a series of older and still largely unresolved North-South political conflicts: the use of policy conditionality, levels of aid financing, and demands for more democratic governance of assistance programs.

These new and old tensions are now the subject of debate on GEF as part of a year-long set of intergovernmental negotiations for restructuring the facility so that it can advance beyond the pilot phase. Although GEF's resources are now small, the negotiations have spurred much interest among governments, aid agencies, and the international environmental community because of its potential to serve as the long-term financial mechanism for the implementation of the biodiversity and climate conventions. In time, GEF's resources may grow substantially. Moreover, GEF reform has broader significance in that the restructuring may embody a new model of programming international assistance that can set the pace for future initiatives to advance sustainable development.

. . . .

ORGANIZING PRINCIPLES OF THE PILOT PHASE

■ GEF WAS FOUNDED ON THE BASIS THAT it would provide concessional finance for the "incremental cost" of projects with global environmental benefits—an approach for environmental grantmaking that is new to development finance. The incremental cost refers to a partial or whole investment in a project that will deliver so-called "global benefits" to the world community—such as establishing a protected area that is rich in biological diversity—but that a developing country would not undertake on its own due to little (short-term) economic incentive to do so. In other words, GEF financing would not be available for projects that are economically viable without the concessional finance, even if the investment contributes in some way to safeguarding the global environment. GEF funds can, nonetheless, be used to cover the difference between national and global benefits. For instance, it might finance the incremental cost to a country of using a less carbon-intensive industrial technology rather than one that is cheaper but more polluting.

In addition, GEF was created with unprecedented flexibility to engage a range of institutions and resources to undertake its mission (see Box 4), but it was purposely denied the apparent extravagance of setting up an independent headquarters. Indeed, one of the most distinctive features of GEF is that three agencies collaborate in its implementation. The World Bank-UNDP-UNEP triad indisputably draws on the key multilateral players in this field, and their respective roles in GEF reflect a conscious effort to bring the best of each into the enterprise.

From the start, GEF's work program was to be fully integrated with the implementing agencies' ongoing operations. Proponents of the arrangement argued that the tight links would help catalyze environmental reform within the big agencies, spur greater interest among aid recipients, and leverage the agencies' far larger volume of resources behind GEF's agenda. Also, the use of the three-way institutional network, with the addition of a very small administrative secretariat, was expected to reduce overhead and the potential duplication of an independent funding entity.

This innovative organizational structure combined with the incremental cost approach proved useful in crafting a political bargain among donors—and, to a lesser extent, developing countries—to support GEF's creation. Donors particularly rallied around the incremental cost concept as a cost-effective way to focus GEF and to contain the demands of developing countries for "new and additional resources." GEF also reso-

BOX 4. HOW THE GEF OPERATES

The World Bank is principally responsible for programming GEF money, implementing most of the projects, and housing the secretariat. The organization also chairs the semiannual GEF meeting of the participants, during which some 30 officials from industrial and developing countries (typically from foreign affairs, environment, and finance ministries) approve policies and projects. The World Bank, with its large administrative, financial, and project management capabilities, has been the dominant partner.

UNDP's responsibilities include providing technical assistance and training, undertaking preinvestment studies and project preparation, and facilitating in-country coordination and prioritization of GEF activities. It is also launching, through its network of Resident Representatives, the $7-million GEF Small Grants Programme (up to $50,000 per grant) mainly for community-based NGOs.

UNEP's role includes setting up and providing support to the Scientific and Technical Advisory Panel (STAP) to advise GEF on strategic planning, formulate scientific and technical criteria for project selection, and review project proposals. STAP also maintains an experts roster to provide support to GEF.

Importantly, the finance mechanism also leverages substantial bilateral contributions beyond support for its core fund. For instance, donors can contribute directly to a particular GEF-managed project and release core funds for other projects. A total of $205 million in co-financing had been pledged as of September 1992, with more than half coming (on concessional rather than grant terms) from Japan. Or, as in the case of the $150 million pledged by United States in the pilot phase, donors can run "parallel" projects (in accordance with GEF criteria) through national aid agencies.

nated with constituencies in industrial countries that were keenly interested in the new fund's agenda. For developing countries, GEF's links to the World Bank and its focus on global issues were problematic, as discussed below, but the availability of new resources and their concessional nature were welcomed.

. . . .
RECASTING THE MODEL

■   WHILE USEFUL IN GETTING THE ORGANIZATION started, the incremental cost approach and institutional arrangements will need to be retooled if GEF is to become effective in its mission to address global environmental threats. Greater attention needs to be given to ensuring that GEF exploits more-strategic and innovative opportunities with its resources as well as strengthens its own identity and particular mission with respect to the implementing agencies.

At the start, GEF participants called for a portfolio of projects that would be well balanced across developing-country regions and across the initial four focal areas in such a way that climate and biodiversity would receive more emphasis (and funds) than international waters and ozone projects. Largely due to pressure to get the organization up and running before the Earth Summit, however, the first projects were largely ones that had been developed earlier by the World Bank; they mainly focused on biodiversity, gave little attention to Africa or to technical assistance, and have generally received low marks for quality and innovation.

Although somewhat uneven, the quality and the geographical and substantive balance of subsequent projects have improved; much less certain, however, is GEF's commitment to testing important new technologies and approaches. A recent World Wildlife Fund study, for instance, found that climate-related energy projects had made relatively little investment in the area of energy efficiency, and that biodiversity projects were weak on participation by local communities.[30] These two approaches should actually be priorities for GEF's climate and biodiversity investments.[31]

A key challenge relating to project quality is the difficulty of translating the incremental cost approach into a workable and effective policy, and serious efforts are under way to clarify and provide guidelines for this. The problem is rooted in the large area of overlap between national and global benefits, and the field of natural resource accounting is simply too new in most cases to quantify environmental gains and losses. The incremental financing could range from 1 to 100 percent of a project, depending on whether it pays for the difference between a power plant fueled by coal versus geothermal energy (which costs more but emits less carbon) or an entire biodiversity reserve. In addition, where training or institutional development is involved, the long-term national benefits of building up local capacity could never be separated out from the global benefits.

At its core, the difficulties with incremental costs really stem from many local and global environmental problems—and effective responses to them—being indistinguishable. This will in practice require that the incremental cost approach be applied on a selective and very flexible basis.

The incremental cost approach is also problematic because it limits GEF's relationship with the implementing agencies, and particularly with the World Bank. A substantial portion of GEF's so-called incremental investment projects is being folded into much larger World Bank lending programs—programs that aim to address a range of objectives that may or, more likely, may not coincide with those of GEF.[32]

For instance, GEF park protection projects are being attached to larger World Bank forestry development programs with more commercial objectives; environmentalists convincingly argue that the negative environmental impacts of the much better financed Bank projects will more than offset the anticipated global benefits of the GEF investment. On the positive side, GEF grants may in some selected cases be a catalyst for pro-environmental reforms in the implementing agencies' ongoing programs.[33]

Given these dynamics, much more attention should be given to ensuring that GEF not be used to cover the environmental costs of projects that ideally should not need concessional financing to control pollution or conserve resources. These objectives should already be imbedded in the agencies' investment strategies. This may mean further development by GEF of admittedly more expensive stand-alone projects and less exploitation of opportunities to "capture the global benefits" of the World Bank's larger investment projects.

Even more challenging is that GEF's focus on projects with global benefits (such as less carbon-intensive energy production or park protection budgets) greatly limits the potential to get at the root causes of environmental problems (like cheap energy prices or agricultural subsidies and land tenure regimes). In many cases, GEF grants may really subsidize investments that cannot be justified on domestic economic terms because the national policy framework is *not* on a sustainable course.

Although it would be a politically sensitive step, GEF will fail unless it moves into the policy arena. Even with limited resources GEF can begin to develop projects that explore the ties between carbon emission levels and policies involving fiscal, monetary, exchange rate, or trade reforms. Or it might finance the technical aspects of environmental policy reforms, such as legal, regulatory, or administrative changes, as part of the expanded role for the U.N. system in national capacity building for sustainable development.

On a bureaucratic level, working relations and coordination among the three implementing agencies has improved with time, but greater efforts to streamline and improve operations are still needed. Each agency processes a GEF project according to its own project cycle requirements. A GEF project attached to a World Bank loan, for instance, must pass through a lengthy and rather torturous process involving nine reviews (ending with the Bank's Executive Board) before it is implemented. Final project approval should rest with the GEF Participants Assembly. Also the Scientific and Technical Advisory Panel (STAP) requires increased support to perform its role effectively. Among STAP's responsibilities is ensuring that GEF projects adhere to specific scientific and technical criteria, but STAP members complained in the pilot phase that their project review responsibilities were inhibited by factors such as the poor quality of project documentation, short deadlines, and lack of administrative and technical support.

Finally, GEF's range of relations with the NGO community seems promising but also needs to be strengthened. Under UNEP auspices, for example, GEF is providing major support for research by the START scientific network described earlier. In addition, numerous local and international NGOs are participating in the execution of GEF technical cooperation and investment projects. Notably, the UNDP-led GEF NGO small grants program is now expanding rapidly with the formation of national committees (composed of government and U.N. officials, NGO leaders, and technical experts) in roughly 30 developing countries to identify investment priorities and select community-level projects. UNDP plans to expand the small grants program as additional resources become available. There are also initial signs of interest for the post-pilot phase GEF to give increased attention to supporting mechanisms for more meaningful participation of affected communities in the design and implementation of projects. This will require developing strong relations with local NGOs.

Less smooth has been GEF's relations with the environmental advocacy NGOs in both North and South. Many of these groups have been pushing for greater access to information and decisionmaking on GEF. The GEF managers have been more open than those in the World Bank to providing project documentation and even to consulting with interested NGOs on policies and projects, but efforts have been uneven. Again, Agenda 21 calls for enhanced NGO consultation in decisions affecting implementation of sustainable development programs, and a permanent GEF should pursue an open information policy and further develop its consultative arrangements with NGOs.

. . . .

NORTH-SOUTH POLITICS OF GEF RESTRUCTURING

■ IN ADDITION TO THE OPERATIONAL CONCERNS identified above, political tensions between industrial and developing countries must be overcome if GEF is to grow into its role as a major permanent financial mechanism for the conventions. Industrial countries like the GEF because of its ties to the World Bank, an institution both respected and controlled by the donors, and because it focuses on the global issues in which they have the greatest collective stake. Developing countries, by contrast, have never been enthusiastic supporters of the facility precisely because they are more concerned with national environmental problems and less trusting of the World Bank.

Developing countries expect their environmental resources to give them greater capacity to command and direct donor financing. They have yet to translate such expectations into tangible political power or into more than small increases in aid financing—a dilemma that is likely to be a continuing source of North-South tension long after the formative stages of GEF.

Developing countries also resent GEF's links to the World Bank because it promises further use of conditions on the flows of aid—in this case environmental ones. They have repeatedly objected to environmental conditionality, arguing that it reduces control over their own natural resources and weakens their right to define their own development and environmental priorities. These concerns are valid, but it is difficult to imagine that a GEF, attached to the World Bank or not, would refrain from using standards related to improved environmental practices in its grant agreements to press for good performance on investment projects.

More immediately serious than these political tensions, however, is the argument by developing countries that GEF's "global" mandate skews international attention and investments away from their more threatening local environmental problems such as poisoned water supplies, health-impairing air pollution, and degrading farmlands. For instance, there are sizable and growing GEF and bilateral resources for preparing climate and biodiversity plans but comparatively little resources to date for financing national sustainable development plans in any of the donor agencies. There is also some evidence that developing countries' small pool of natural resource/environment managers and scientists are shifting into the global environmental set of issues because of the availability of international funds. This undermines the ability to strengthen developing-country capabilities to address national sustainable development.

In this regard, it is a positive step that developing countries had some limited success in broadening the substantive scope of the GEF beyond the initial four focal areas. GEF participants agreed just prior to UNCED to add land degradation issues such as desertification and deforestation—but only "as they relate to the four focal areas"—to the list of global concerns available for financing. Especially in the case of desertification, this allows GEF to become more active in what many consider to be more a regional than a global issue; it also allows broader scope for participation by African countries, which had been underrepresented in earlier GEF projects.

. . . .
UNFINISHED BUSINESS

■ BOTH THE CLIMATE AND THE BIODIVERSITY conventions designate GEF as the interim financial entity for supporting developing-country participation in their activities. Developing countries wisely inserted language into the two conventions that establishes this arrangement only on an interim basis until more is certain about the structure of GEF beyond its pilot stage. They are especially concerned about future voting arrangements, GEF's ties to the three implementing agencies, and the relationship with the two conferences of the parties for the biodiversity and climate conventions.

The GEF replenishment negotiations will be greatly influenced by progress on these issues. Developing countries had high hopes that UNCED would spur major multilateral aid increases, but only the tiny GEF was given reasonable prospects that its budget would be significantly expanded after the summit. In Rio, the heads of state from both the United Kingdom and Germany called for a doubling or tripling in the facility's budget. Tripling to a $1 billion annual budget will be especially vital if GEF is to be able to explore the policy implications of its mission and effectively broaden its thematic scope to address more regional issues.

To smooth the way for the completion of the climate and biodiversity conventions, GEF participants agreed prior to UNCED to devise a "more democratic" governance structure. But the terms remain to be decided. When contentious issues arise and the Participant's Assembly cannot reach a decision by consensus, developing countries would like to see a "double majority" voting formula that requires a majority within each of two constituency groups—the donors and the developing countries. This would give veto power to recipient countries as well as donors, an arrangement that would be unprecedented for a Bretton Woods financial institution but that is not unknown in the U.N. system. Most of the donor countries, not surprisingly, tend to support a World Bank-style voting formula for GEF, weighted according to financial contributions. This sense of ownership and control on the part of donors is a key factor explaining the expanding mandate and resources of the international financial institutions over the last several years relative to U.N. agencies. In the spirit of compromise, innovative proposals on the table well worth considering would allow use of the double-majority voting system but would give proportionally larger shares in the donor constituency according to levels of financial contribution.

Resolving how GEF is to relate to the conferences of the parties to the biodiversity and climate conventions—and, by extension, to the implementing agencies—promises to be as thorny as reaching agreement on the voting procedures. Following the precedent set by the Montreal Protocol on ozone-depleting substances, negotiators for the two new conventions agreed to distance the operations of GEF from the World Bank by introducing text that explicitly leaves control over the financing mechanism's "policies, program priorities, and eligibility criteria" to their respective conferences.

One GEF observer notes that "the independence of the conventions ensures a separation of powers between their conferences of parties and the GEF."[34] Potentially, this separation could contribute to greater accountability, as the conferences will be reviewing the performance of the GEF on an ongoing basis. In addition, STAP is expected to provide a "scientific link" to the conferences. Also, like the Commission on Sustainable Development, the engagement of the conferences in development assistance issues will provide another high-level forum for negotiation and reaching agreement on priority areas for capacity building, project investment, and policy reforms. Nevertheless, there should be caution with investing too many aid decisions in the conferences of the parties given their "least-common-denominator" approach to decisionmaking. The participating delegations at the conferences are typically from foreign affairs ministries and can be weak on technical and/or aid-programming expertise. Clearly, management of GEF would be impeded if the large conferences, or even designated working groups, became too closely involved in its day-to-day operations.

No doubt anticipating these problems, GEF participants endorsed the notion that a post-pilot phase Participants Assembly would ensure that GEF adheres to the conventions' policy and strategic directions; continue to direct, oversee, and coordinate GEF work programs; and provide periodic reports to the conventions. This division of labor seems sensible and is calculated to reassure the conferences, especially because they can in theory decide to fire GEF as the financial mechanism if it does not perform adequately.

Indeed, in response to the operational and political problems besetting GEF, there have been proposals to make its secretariat fully independent of the implementing agencies. While worth careful consideration, the proposal has sizable drawbacks, such as a substantial rise in overhead costs and greater isolation of environmental assistance efforts within the development system. Calls for an independent secretariat would also likely be strongly resisted by donors and hence adversely affect GEF's replenishment prospects.

Nevertheless, greater autonomy for GEF—including procedures for a more streamlined project cycle that invests final project approval decisions with the Participants Assembly—would better enable it to undertake the reforms identified above and to be responsive to the interests of the parties of the conventions. Additionally, GEF requires a somewhat expanded secretariat with greater technical and coordinating capacity to further improve project quality and enhance STAP's oversight role.

To conclude, the incremental cost approach and innovative collaborative institutional model proved effective in getting GEF off the ground quickly but these principles require reformulation in the post-pilot phase to allow the fund to search for and invest in lasting solutions to global environmental threats. These changes should include:

- Application of the incremental cost approach on a very selective and flexible basis in recognition that addressing global problems cannot be entirely divorced from the kinds of measures required to improve management of local environmental problems.

- Greater emphasis on strategic and innovative investment projects, particularly in the areas of energy efficiency for climate protection and meaningful community participation in biodiversity conservation.

- Commitment to building consensus and investing in the range of macroeconomic and sectoral policy reforms that will be pivotal to effective responses to the global threats. GEF should explore research and demonstration projects on the relationship between policy reforms and sustainable resource management within its thematic areas as well as support the technical aspects of legal, regulatory, and administrative policy reforms.

- Greater autonomy for GEF's operational policies and governing procedures from the three implementing agencies. The secretariat's technical and coordinating capacity must be expanded to improve project quality and streamline the project cycle. The secretariat should also support enhanced STAP involvement in project development and monitoring. It should be the exception rather than the rule that GEF project financing is subsumed within much larger World Bank lending programs that do not have global environmental concerns as their main objective.

■ Continued strengthening of GEF relations with scientific, environmental, and operating NGOs, particularly in developing countries. The post-pilot phase GEF should also remain committed to an open information policy and should improve consultative arrangements with NGOs.

Part VI

Conclusion

■ THE EARTH SUMMIT DRAMATIZED THE NECESSITY of shifting from conventional development strategies that seek to repair environmental damage to integrated strategies that prevent or at least minimize environmental degradation. And Agenda 21, which was its culmination, provides an action plan for redirecting development on an environmentally sustainable basis.

Many nations are—to varying degrees—undertaking to change conventional patterns of production and consumption because of concerns that environmental degradation is becoming an increasingly serious constraint on development objectives and may actually reach irreversible thresholds that damage the earth's ecosystems. Developing nations face a particularly difficult task in their transition to sustainable development. They must change the course of conventional development while accelerating economic growth to meet essential needs and do it with maximum efficiency in the use of scarce and inadequate financial resources.

As pointed out in this *Policy Essay*, the institutional means for helping nations carry out the Earth Summit's agenda are of critical importance. Steps must be taken to ensure that governments are up to the challenge, through new institutions if necessary but preferably through adapting existing ones. The new Commission on Sustainable Development can and should contribute significantly to building support of governments and monitoring overall progress. Its effectiveness will depend on dedicated leadership, an efficient secretariat, and public support in major countries.

In general, the goals of environmentally sustainable development must be pursued in ongoing investment and development programs and by the national and international institutions directly involved. It is in this context that the roles of the World Bank, UNDP, and UNEP assume special importance. Taken together, they constitute the key functional multilateral components for helping nations achieve environmentally prudent development. Each of these key agencies needs some institutional strengthening, however, to ensure effectiveness in its respective role.

The World Bank is well advanced in strengthening staff capabilities and adopting appropriate policies and procedures for incorporating sustainable development in its operations, but their fully effective application is still in process. UNDP is at an early stage of building and redirecting its institutional capabilities for environmental development assistance. UNEP has achieved a sound programmatic foundation for environmental assessment and advice, one that now requires substantial improvement and expansion.

The close operational collaboration of these three key institutions assumes increased importance, for sustainable development is inherently a process that demands an integrated application of functional inputs—capital investment, technical capacity building and training, and scientifically sound assessments. Each of the three multilateral institutions depends, in part, on the work of the other two for achieving the best results in fulfillment of its role. GEF, in beginning to address selected global environmental threats and their relation to national programs, has demonstrated both the importance and the difficulties of this interagency collaboration.

The proposed national sustainable development strategies of developing countries—incorporating the World Bank-sponsored environment action plans—provide the basis for dialogue with donors on their implementation. As these strategies become operational, increased funding should be made available. Donor support for the participatory and community engagement of people and their organizations is as important as well-prepared sustainable development strategies at the national level. Ultimately, caring for and sustaining the health of the earth—with its variety of species, aesthetic pleasures, and productive potential—depends on people and the influence they bring to bear on governments and international agencies.

Notes

[1] Organisation for Economic Co-operation and Development (OECD), Development Assistance Committee, *Development Co-operation 1992*, (Paris: OECD, 1992), p. 78.

[2] World Commission on Environment and Development, *Our Common Future* (Oxford: Oxford University Press, 1987), p. 8.

[3] United Nations Conference on Environment and Development (UNCED), "Rio Declaration on Environment and Development" (New York: United Nations, 1992).

[4] OECD, *Development Co-operation 1990* (Paris: OECD, 1990), p. 29.

[5] Nitin Desai, "The Outcome of Rio," in *NETWORK '92*, No. 18 (Geneva: The Centre for Our Common Future, June-July 1992), p. 18.

[6] UNCED, *Agenda 21* (New York: United Nations, 1992), Chapter 4, para. 4.11.

[7] "Rio Declaration," op. cit.

[8] *Agenda 21*, op. cit., Chapter 37, para. 37.7.

[9] Ibid.

[10] In addition to providing back-up for the Commission, the secretariat will also support the efforts of two closely related U.N. bodies concerned with the implementation of Agenda 21: the Inter-Agency Committee on Sustainable Development (which reports to the Agency Coordinating Committee) will coordinate compliance in the U.N. system; and the new High-level Advisory Board of scientific, business, and other nongovernmental leaders will provide expert advice to the Secretary General.

[11] The real monitoring for the conventions' implementation will take place in the respective parties of the conventions.

[12] Report of the Secretary-General, "Institutional Arrangements to Follow-up the United Nations Conference on Environment and Development," prepared for the 47th Session of the General Assembly, New York, October 1992, p. 13.

[13] Robert O. Keohane, Peter M. Haas, and Marc A. Levy, "The Effectiveness of International Environmental Institutions," in *Institutions for the Earth: Sources of Effective International Environmental Protection*, Haas, Keohane, and Levy, eds. (Cambridge, MA: The MIT Press, 1993) p. 14.

[14] Among the specialized agencies active in the execution of environmentally related technical cooperation projects are the Food and Agriculture Organization (FAO), the United Nations Education, Scientific, and Cultural Organization (UNESCO), the International Maritime Organization (IMO), the World Meteorological Organization (WMO), and the United Nations Industrial Development Organization (UNIDO). The United Nations Conference on Trade and Development (UNCTAD) has an important role in trade and technology assessments.

[15] Report of the Administrator, "Environment and Development" (New York: UNDP, 1993), No. 3, p. 10.

[16] Konrad von Moltke and Ginny Eckert, "The United Nations Development Programme and the Environment: A Nongovernmental Assessment," World Wildlife Fund unpublished paper, (January 5, 1991).

[17] "The Follow-up to UNCED: UNDP's Strategy in Support of Sustainable Development," UNDP Governing Council Paper, June 1993 Session, United Nations, New York.

[18] Statement by Dr. Mostafa Tolba, Executive Director of UNEP, to the Sixth Session of the Committee of International Development Institutions on Environment, Washington, DC, 1985.

[19] Public Law 99-190 in 1985.

[20] Public Law 101-240 in 1989.

[21] Chairman Bradford Morse, *Sardar Sardovar: Report of the Independent Review* (Ottawa: Resources Futures International, Inc., 1992), p. xxiv.

[22] World Bank, *The World Bank and the Environment: A Progress Report*, World Bank Report (Washington, DC: World Bank, 1992), p. 4.

[23] Ibid., p. 66.

[24] David Reed, ed., *Structural Adjustment and the Environment* (Boulder, CO: Westview Press for WWF International, 1992).

[25] World Bank, *World Development Report 1992* (New York: Oxford University Press, 1992).

[26] *The World Bank and the Environment*, op. cit., p. 28.

[27] Willi A. Wapenhans, et al., "Report of the Portfolio Management Task Force," World Bank document, July 1, 1992, p. 1.

[28] "Summary Proceedings of Conference with Borrowers," in Wapenhans, *Report of the World Bank Task Force on Portfolio Management*, op. cit., Annex B.

[29] *The World Bank and the Environment*, op. cit., p. 20.

[30] David Reed, ed., *The Global Environmental Facility: Sharing Responsibility for the Biosphere*, Vol. II (Washington, DC: World Wildlife Fund with World Wide Fund for Nature, International, 1993).

[31] For a discussion of the importance of energy conservation to climate programs and of community-based approaches to biodiversity/forestry programs, see Patti L. Petesch, *North-South Environmental Strategies, Costs, and Bargains*, Policy Essay No. 5 (Washington, DC: Overseas Development Council, 1992), Parts II and III.

[32] Of the GEF investment projects—which the World Bank executes—64 percent (or 34 out of a total of 53 projects) are associated with larger World Bank projects. When including UNEP research and UNDP technical assistance projects (all stand-alone projects), 30 percent of all GEF projects are associated with larger World Bank loans. Nicholas van Praag, Global Environment Facility, Washington, DC, personal communication, April 12, 1993.

[33] For instance, the nongovernmental International Institute for Energy Conservation worked with the World Bank in preparing a major GEF-OECF (Japan) energy conservation project for Thailand that includes substantial investments in a demand-side management program. This is significant given the World Bank's traditional focus on supply-side energy approaches despite the substantial savings that can be gained from demand-side interventions. More

important in the long run, the Bank staff learned much in preparing the project, which may lead to its replication in other countries as part of the agency's normal energy lending operations. Michael Philips, personal communication, March 31, 1993.

[34] Richard N. Mott, "The Global Environment Facility and Mechanisms for Financial Transfers Under the United Nations Framework Convention on Climate Change and the Convention on Biological Diversity," World Wildlife Fund, Washington DC, undated memorandum.

Annex:
A Brief Guide to
Agenda 21

Chapter 1: Preamble. The new global partnerships for sustainable development begin with member governments' own national strategies, plans, policies, and processes.

Chapter 2: International Cooperation. Protectionism and other obstacles to international trade should be reduced by both international and domestic measures. Trade and environmental policies should become mutually supportive. Financial resources should be enhanced through action in the fields of private and nonconcessional flows, and official development assistance (ODA) and debt. Member governments should make efforts to improve mobilization and allocation of domestic resources.

Chapter 3: Combatting Poverty. The struggle against poverty is the shared responsibility of all countries. Each country should pursue a sustainable growth strategy, taking direct action to eradicate poverty. Strategies should be developed with participation of all parts of society. The United Nations should make poverty alleviation a major priority.

Chapter 4: Changing Consumption Patterns. Industrial-country consumption patterns must shift to reduce environmental stress even as developing countries increase consumption to meet food, health-care, shelter, and educational needs. Recognizing that this represents a fresh area for analysis, private and public organizations need to make a concerted effort to understand the issues. Meanwhile, each member should adopt measures to achieve more efficient use of energy and resources, to minimize generation of wastes, and to assist households to make environmentally sound purchasing decisions. Measures can include improvements of government purchasing, reflection of environmental costs in pricing, and promotion of new attitudes.

Chapter 5: Demographic Dynamics. More needs to be known about the relationships among demographic dynamics, technology, cultural behavior, natural resources, and life-support systems. Demographic factors need to be taken into account in planning. Population programs should be developed that integrate demographic trends with health, technology, human settlements, socio-economic structures, and access to resources. Inter alia, member governments should assure provision of safe and effective reproductive health care and affordable, accessible services for responsible planning of family size. The U.N. Fund for Population Activities should work with developing countries and others to achieve coordination of population assistance to assure that recipient strategies are adequately funded.

Chapter 6: Protecting and Promoting Human Health. Five programs deal with primary health care, communicable diseases, vulnerable groups, urban health, and risks from environmental pollution and hazards. The international community had earlier adopted a number of specific goals to be achieved by the year 2000, which are reiterated. Action is required by member governments and a number of international organizations.

Chapter 7: Human Settlements. The eight programs in this chapter compose an "enabling" strategy for dealing with human settlements, primarily in urban areas. Although urbanization is accompanied by problems, it also is an opportunity for efficiently organizing services. For this, better planning and management will be required along with policies that encourage household investments. Major public investments will be required for water, sanitation, drainage, solid waste management, energy, and transportation. These must be designed for both environmental and financial sustainability.

Chapter 8: Integrating Environment and Development in Decisionmaking. The four programs deal with planning, law, and regulation, use of economic instruments and accounting.

Chapter 9: Protection of the Atmosphere. Four programs cover actions to improve understanding of atmospheric systems and to deal with specific sectors such as energy, transportation, ozone depletion, and transboundary atmospheric pollution. Most actions will be by member governments and private entities.

Chapter 10: Land Resources Planning and Management. Land use decisions are influenced primarily by national and local governments and by private activities. Efficient land use will become increasingly important as higher production levels and more population compete for finite land resources.

Chapter 11: Combating Deforestation. Four programs address forestry issues. Forestry principles were separately negotiated at Rio. Both the climate and biological diversity conventions also address the issue. One program concentrates on better data, improved planning, more training, and effective coordination. Another calls for strengthening the Tropical Forestry Action Programme. The third program addresses evaluation issues and the fourth, capacity building.

Chapter 12: Desertification. Six programs give priority to prevention of further land degradation in dry areas. They would strengthen the information base, encourage soil conservation (including through afforestation), seek alternative livelihoods, develop anti-desertification programs, undertake drought preparedness schemes, and encourage knowledge and participation. The key recommendation is for the negotiation of a convention to focus on countries, particularly in Africa, where desertification is an important issue.

Chapter 13: Sustainable Mountain Development. Two programs address information and watershed management. In addition to national action, regional groups that encourage improved planning and information exchange are encouraged. One example is the International Center for Integrated Mountain Development, which works in Asia.

Chapter 14: Promoting Sustainable Agriculture and Rural Development. This chapter reminds us that a doubled world population must be fed largely through improved use of already cultivated high potential lands while conserving and rehabilitating lands in more fragile ecosystems. Twelve programs address the issue. Each member is urged to improve its policy framework for sustainable agriculture and rural development. Other programs address issues of participation, off-farm development, land resources, conservation, water, genetic resources, pest management, plant nutrition, energy, and the effects of ultraviolet radiation.

Chapter 15: Conservation of Biological Diversity. This chapter complements the new convention and urges that the convention come into force as soon as possible. At the same time, each member should develop its own strategy for conservation and sustainable use of biological resources.

Chapter 16: Biotechnology. Five programs address issues in agriculture, health, environment, safety, and institutional capacity. Most action will be at the national level, but many international agencies will play a role.

Chapter 17: Oceans and Seas. Seven programs address coastal area development, marine living resources (in the high seas and under national jurisdiction), climate change, coordination, and small-island development. Most activities will be at the national level, but international cooperation is essential. Regional commissions might work with governments in developing and reviewing national strategies. The Convention on the Law of the Sea should be reviewed by member governments to facilitate its early entry into force with wide participation. Early agreements on high-seas fishing issues is important.

Chapter 18: Freshwater. Seven programs address integrated water planning, water resources assessment, protection, supply and sanitation, urban water, agricultural water, and the impacts of climate change. The theme is holistic management for irrigation, industrial, and domestic uses. National plans should be developed by year 2000.

Chapter 19: Toxic Chemicals. Six programs cover assessments, classification and labeling, risk reduction, capacity building, and trade. Overall coordination is through the International Panel on Chemical Safety, a joint activity of the World Health Organization, the U.N. Environment Programme, and the International Labour Office. An intergovernmental meeting should be convened in 1993 by the three agencies.

Chapter 20: Hazardous Wastes. Four programs address life-cycle management to reduce hazardous waste production, to increase training, and to deal with issues of transboundary movements including illegal traffic. Inter alia, governments should bring into force and implement the Basel and Bamako Conventions.

Chapter 21: Solid Wastes. Four programs address waste minimization, reuse, environmentally sound disposal, and extension of waste-service coverage.

Chapter 22: Radioactive Wastes. The program seeks to promote safe and sound management of radioactive wastes.

Chapter 23. This is an introduction to Chapters 24-32, which address the strengthening of the role of major groups. It stresses the theme of participation. The chapters benefited from contributions by representatives of the groups involved.

Chapter 24: Women in Development. Even though the need to fully involve women as participants and beneficiaries in the development process is recognized in many other Agenda 21 chapters, this chapter brings together woman-specific issues. It urges implementation of the Nairobi Forward-Looking Strategies for the Advancement of Women as well as a number of conventions. A world conference on women's issues is scheduled to be held in Beijing in September 1995 affording an opportunity for stock-taking.

Chapter 25: Children and Youth. Two programs address issues of youth and children. Participation by youth in decisionmaking processes is emphasized.

Chapter 26: Indigenous People. This chapter gives recognition to the holistic traditional knowledge that indigenous peoples bring to natural resource and environmental issues. Their involvement in the national and international processes is underlined by the fact that 1993 is the International Year for the World's Indigenous People.

Chapter 27: Nongovernmental Organizations (NGOs). With UNCED, the NGOs gained increased opportunities for participation. This reflected their growing number and importance and their critical role in society. The chapter encourages considerably greater involvement within member countries and in international organizations.

Chapter 28: Local Authorities. Local communities play a very important role in mobilizing households and providing services relevant to sustainable development issues. The Summit called upon local authorities each to develop an Agenda 21 process in consultation with citizens.

Chapter 29: Workers and Their Trade Unions. The chapter stresses the need for workers and their representatives to participate in sustainable development activities.

Chapter 30: Business and Industry. Two programs focus on cleaner production and the promotion of responsible entrepreneurship.

Chapter 31: The Scientific and Technological Community. Two programs address the need to improve communication and cooperation among scientific and technological community decisionmakers and the public, and to improve and promote international acceptance of codes of practice and guidelines related to science and technology.

Chapter 32: Farmers. This chapter reflects the importance of participation of farmers and their representatives in sustainable development activities.

Chapter 33: Financial Resources and Mechanisms. The chapter addresses the need for increased funding to implement developing countries' plan for sustainable development. There is general agreement to make progress toward the U.N. target of 0.7 percent of GNP for ODA. The needs and roles of multilateral development banks and funds, U.N. bodies, capacity-building institutions, bilateral assistance, debt relief and private funding are discussed, as is the need to encourage foreign direct investment and technology transfer. New ways of generating resources should be explored, including new forms of debt relief, use of economic and fiscal measures, the feasibility of tradable permits, new schemes for private fundraising, and the reallocation of resources presently committed to military purposes. The concept of an evolving partnership among all countries that links developing-country sustainable development strategies with enhanced and predictable levels of funding is introduced. The chapter underlines the importance of regular review and monitoring of the adequacy of funding and mechanisms.

Chapter 34: Technology Transfer. The chapter highlights the importance of technology to developing countries, reviewing a number of things that might be done to facilitate its availability.

Chapter 35: Science. Four programs address strengthening the scientific base and improving understanding of Earth's carrying capacity.

Chapter 36: Education. Three programs encourage implementation of the recommendations of the 1990 World Conference on Education for All, promotion of public awareness of sustainable development issues and steps to increase training activity.

Chapter 37: Capacity Building. The chapter calls for national capacity-building strategies, technical cooperation in the context of long-term sector or subsector capacity building strategies, a review of the whole system of technical cooperation, improvements in the U.N. systems' contributions to capacity building, and exploration of possible regional initiatives in this field, including peer-country exchanges of experience.

Chapter 38: International Institutional Arrangements. This chapter includes recommendations for the follow-up of UNCED by the General

Assembly and the Economic and Social Council. A comprehensive review of Agenda 21 in a special session of the General Assembly is scheduled for 1997.

Chapter 39: International Legal Instruments and Mechanisms. In this chapter, members suggest measures to assess the effectiveness of international agreements and to set priorities for future law-making on sustainable development issues. There is special concern for making developing-country participation in agreements more effective and for developing improved dispute settlement mechanisms.

Chapter 40: Information for Decisionmaking. Two programs address the need to improve data availability. It is proposed to develop improved indicators of sustainable development. UNEP's Earthwatch would be strengthened, as would the capacity of national and international organizations to network effectively.

Source: Joseph Wheeler, prepared for the Earth Council, San José, Costa Rica. The paper was written as a basis for discussion and does not reflect the views of the Earth Council or its Organizing Committee.

About the Authors

MAURICE J. WILLIAMS is president of the Society for International Development (SID), editor of the SID journal *Development*, and ODC senior associate. He was executive director of the U.N. World Food Council (1978–1985), chair of the OECD Development Assistance Committee (1974–78), deputy administrator of USAID (1970–74), and assistant administrator of USAID for South Asia and Near East (1967–1970). He was advisor to the U.N. Secretary-General for UNCED and a founder of the Earth Council. His publications include *U.S. Development Cooperation Policies, Aid Coordination and Effectiveness,* and *U.N. Programs for Technical Assistance in Africa.*

PATTI L. PETESCH joined the Poverty and Environment Program of the Overseas Development Council in 1987. She has published studies and articles on the environment and the developing countries, including articles on the issues of urban environmental problems, tropical deforestation, and the links between trade and the environment. In addition, Ms. Petesch authored the 1992 ODC Policy Essay, *North-South Environmental Strategies, Costs, and Bargains.*

About the ODC

ODC fosters an understanding of how development relates to a much changed U.S. domestic and international policy agenda and helps shape the new course of global development cooperation.

ODC's programs focus on three main issues: the challenge of political and economic transitions and the reform of development assistance programs; the development dimensions of international global problems; and the implications of development for U.S. economic security.

In pursuing these themes, ODC functions as:

■ *A center for policy analysis.* Bridging the worlds of ideas and actions, ODC translates the best academic research and analysis on selected issues of policy importance into information and recommendations for policymakers in the public and private sectors.

■ *A forum for the exchange of ideas.* ODC's conferences, seminars, workshops, briefings bring together legislators, business executives, scholars, and representatives of international financial institutions and nongovernmental groups.

■ *A resource for public education.* Through its publications, meetings, testimony, lectures, and formal and informal networking, ODC makes timely, objective, nonpartisan information available to an audience that includes but reaches far beyond the Washington policymaking community.

ODC is a private, nonprofit organization funded by foundations, corporations, governments, and private individuals.

Stephen J. Friedman is the Chairman of the Overseas Development Council, and John W. Sewell is the Council's President.

Board of Directors

Overseas Development Council
SPECIAL PUBLICATIONS SUBSCRIPTION OFFER
Policy Essays • Policy Focus

As a subscriber to the ODC's 1993 publication series, you will have access to an invaluable source of independent analyses of U.S.-Third World issues—economic, political, and social—at a savings of at least 10% off the regular price.

Brief and easy-to-read, each **Policy Focus** briefing paper provides background information and analysis on a current topic on the policy agenda. In 1993, 6–8 papers will cover the Bretton Woods institutions and the former Soviet Union, the Global Environment Facility, the Generalized System of Preferences, and the implications of the North American Free Trade Area, among other topics.

Policy Essays explore critical issues on the U.S.-Third World agenda in 80-120 succinct pages, offering concrete recommendations for action. The two final essays in the "conditionality" series, *Pro-Poor Aid Conditionality* and *Global Goals, Contentious Means: Issues of Multiple Aid Conditionality*, explore the potential utility of applying conditionality for the goal of poverty reduction and the implications of multiple aid conditionality—linking political, environmental, military, and pro-poor reforms to foreign aid.

Sustaining the Earth: Role for Multilateral Development Institutions will assess the international institutional capabilities that now exist for carrying through on the UNCED commitments of sustainable development.

United States and Africa: Into the 21st Century examines the pressing regional challenges of ending civil conflict, expanding and consolidating democracy, and achieving economic recovery and sustainable growth. It also assesses options for future U.S. policy.

SUBSCRIPTION OPTIONS

Special Publications Subscription Offer*	$65.00
(all Policy Essays (5–6) and Policy Focus briefing papers (6–8) issued in 1993)	
1993 Policy Essay Subscription*	$50.00
Policy Focus Subscription*	$20.00

* Subscribers will receive all 1993 publications issued to date upon receipt of payment; other publications in subscription will be sent upon release. Book-rate postage is included in price.

All orders require prepayment. Visa and Mastercard orders accepted by phone or mail. Please send check or money order to:

Publication Orders
Overseas Development Council
1875 Connecticut Avenue, NW
Suite 1012
Washington, DC 20009
(202) 234-8701

O | D | C

POLICY ESSAY NO. 9